Revised Edition
Learning At Home:
A Mother's Guide To
Homeschooling

By
Marty Layne

Marty Layne

Sea Change Publications
Victoria, B.C.
Canada

Please note:
    Before starting to homeschool, check with your provincial or state education department for regulations applying to homeschooling. These regulations vary from place to place. This book does not address the legal implications or requirements of homeschooling. The author assumes no responsibility for any action taken regarding homeschooling. Readers should find out what is legally required to homeschool in the area in which they live.

Revised Edition
Learning At Home: A Mother's Guide to Homeschooling

Published by:
Sea Change Publications
1850 San Lorenzo Ave.
Victoria, B. C. V8N 2E9 Canada

03 02 01 00   5 4 3

ISBN 0-9682938-2-4
Canadian Cataloguing in Publication
Layne, Marty, 1948-
  Learning at home

  Includes bibliographical references.
  ISBN 0-9682938-2-4
  1. Home schooling. I. Title.
LC40.L39 2000   371.04'2   C00-910582-4

Dedicated to
my children - Josh, Noah, Robin, and Holly -
my husband - Larry -
and in memoriam to
Henry C. Layne (1907 -1988)

To order copies of this book:

Write or call: Sea Change Publications
1850 San Lorenzo Ave.
Victoria, B.C. V8N 2E9
Canada   250-477-0173
email: seachangepublications@home.com

Price per book:
   US funds $13.95 plus $2.00 shipping and handling
   Canadian funds $17.95 plus $2.00 shipping and handling
      (volume discounts available, please inquire)

To contact the author:

Marty Layne provides workshops and seminars for those interested in learning more about homeschooling. Inquiries about her availability should be directed care of the publisher at the address below. The author welcomes comments and suggestions for future editions of this book.

   Marty Layne
   Sea Change Publications
   1850 San Lorenzo Ave.
   Victoria, B.C. V8N 2E9 Canada
   http://members.home.net/seachangepublications
   email: seachangepublications@home.com

<u>CONTENTS</u>

Photo credits:
Front cover and pages 122, 152, & 164 Larry Layne
Pages 11, 80, 94, 134, 145, 152, 158, 180, 181, & 189 Marty Layne
Back cover Noah Layne

INTRODUCTION

This book is written from a mother's point of view. I started writing this book in 1995. It took me three years to complete and publish the first edition. It took me three years to complete because I was writing in "mother time." My writing took place in odd times, in odd places, and in spurts. I enjoyed the whole process. Two years later, I published the revised edition. This edition has some new material incorporated into the first edition. I still work in "mother time" proofreading while my daughter is at a dance class or as I am waiting for the bread to be finished baking in the oven.

Mothering and homeschooling continue to give me a chance to develop myself in ways that I could never have imagined before I started. In Western culture, freedom from child caring responsibilities is often seen as the best and only way for a mother to continue to develop herself. I couldn't disagree more. The time I have spent being at home, playing and learning with my children, has been the most productive period of my life. No pun intended!

My experience as a homeschooling mother has helped me to appreciate the importance of relationships and to value the interdependence of children and their mothers. At a time when we in the Western world are lurching along trying to reconcile our way of life with the ecological effects it has on the whole planet, an opportunity to explore the issue of interdependence in rearing children may seem to be irrelevant. However, until we treat children with the care, love, and respect that is their birth right, we cannot learn to treat the earth that way.

My decision in my early twenties to move to a farm in Cape Breton, Nova Scotia was a move toward ecologically sound living practices. It was also an attempt to become independent. The five years I spent attempting to live as a self-sufficient farmer showed me how impossible it is to live independently. We need so many things we cannot provide for ourselves - everything from metals that are dug and smelted to communication tools - that to have independence as a goal is simplistic and impossible. Because of that experience, I approached motherhood with an appreciation of interdependence that has been invaluable in rearing my children.

As you will read about in the following chapters, this book is not intended to convince anyone that homeschooling is the only way of educating children. It is as much about establishing good relationships with children as about educating them. Therefore, it can be read by any mother, regardless of her choice of education for her children, and be helpful. Fathers, too, will find it informative.

If you are curious about homeschooling and wonder if it is something you could do, read on.

If you have a friend, relative, or neighbor who is homeschooling, this book can give you some insight as to why someone would choose this method of education.

If you are a teacher, you might find the idea of homeschooling uncomfortable. I hope that this book can help you to see that when someone chooses to homeschool, it is not a condemnation of the teaching profession. Instead, homeschooling parents can be seen as a source of ideas and insights about how children learn for we have the opportunity to work one on one with children that few teachers have.

If you are a parent who is pleased with the way school is working for your family and are interested in providing learning opportunities for your child in your home, this book can give you some ideas to use to supplement your child's education.

My husband, Larry, and I have four children - Josh born in 1977, Noah born in 1979, Robin born in 1982, and Holly born in 1985. They have been learning at home since they were born.

This book is a compilation of the things we have done in our family as our children have gained mastery of the three "R's"; things I have heard or read about that others have done when homeschooling; my thoughts and observations about the effects of homeschooling; and suggestions about how to do it. It is meant as a guide to give you an idea of what homeschooling might be like. It is not meant as the definition of how all homeschooling should be done.

I wrote this book in response to the many requests for information about homeschooling I have received. It was written to inform, support, and encourage anyone considering homeschooling as well as to provide new ideas and directions, support, and encouragement for those who are already homeschooling.

Homeschooling has proved to be successful for many. However, like any other method of educating children, there are no guarantees. We can never know the outcome before we start. Each child brings a different gift to this planet Earth. Homeschooling will not make a child become a musical genius or a computer whiz. No method of education can turn a tulip into a daffodil. However, homeschooling can help you to nurture your children so that they will grow to be themselves. And as a side benefit, homeschooling can also help you become more aware of your own gifts and talents.

CHAPTER 1
Can I Do This - Teach My Child At Home?

The characteristics it takes to homeschool
How to acquire those characteristics

Before I list the characteristics which I think are important in order to be able to teach your child at home, let me define what I mean by teaching. *The New Lexicon Webster's Encyclopedic Dictionary of the English Language, Canadian Edition* lists four definitions for teach, three of which I quote "to give instruction to, to train; to give to another knowledge or skill which one has oneself; to cause to understand." With this as a basis, I extend this definition to also mean being aware of when the child is ready to receive the teaching. In other words, just because I am ready to give my child instruction in reading doesn't mean my child is ready or able to receive it.

When I teach, I try to be aware of my child's ability, readiness, and desire to learn a particular subject; to be sensitive to my child's motivation; and to be aware of my own motivation in wanting to teach a particular something to my child. Teaching can only happen when there is someone willing to be the learner as well as someone willing to be the teacher. The method used to instruct needs to be suitable to the person receiving the instruction.

With this definition of teaching in mind, I have drawn up a list of characteristics that I think are important to have in order to succeed at teaching your child at home. As you read through the list keep in mind that the first characteristic is something that you must have to start with, the others can be acquired and developed over time.

To succeed at homeschooling you need to:

1. Genuinely like your child or children and enjoy his, her, or their company

2. Have a sense of humor

3. Be able to read, write and do basic math and be willing to upgrade your skills as necessary

4. Have a commitment to a philosophy that leads you to homeschool

5. Be willing to develop communication/listening skills

6. Be prepared to receive criticism for your decision to homeschool

7. Have a support system or network and/or a supportive partner

8. Be able to learn from mistakes

9. Be willing to develop limit setting skills

10. Be willing to develop patience

11. Be willing to develop observational skills

12. Be willing to change

1. Genuinely like your child or children and enjoy his, her, or their company

Although it may seem rather obvious, this characteristic is sometimes overlooked. I think it's the most important one. What does it mean to like your child? It means that you enjoy being with your child. You take delight in her presence. You enjoy listening to her tell you things, you enjoy observing how she learns new skills, you are pleased to be in relationship with your child. This may seem simplistic, but it's so important.

If your child is going to spend most of her waking hours in your company, it's vital to her well being that you enjoy the daily interaction between you. This doesn't mean that there won't be moments when you need peace and quiet and some time to yourself. However, if you are frequently resentful of your child's need for you and you are constantly irritated by your children's presence, homeschooling your children will not work for you.

Being with children all the time is not easy. Children's needs can bring up all sorts of unresolved personal problems for their parents. The more willing you are as an adult to face your own personal issues and own them, the more able you are to be in relationship with your child as he or she is rather than as you imagine he or she should be.

I enjoyed being with my children as they grew. I enjoyed watching them play when they were little. I enjoyed their creativity and inventiveness. Observing my children gain mastery of many skills such as reading, dancing, or playing an instrument has been one of my greatest pleasures as a homeschooling mother.

If you have enjoyed being home with your preschool children, and the thought of sending your 5 year old off to kindergarten makes you sad, you are someone who could homeschool. If you are a mom who has sent her children to school, spends a lot of time in the local elementary school helping in your children's classes, and are beginning to wonder why you're spending so much time with other people's children, you might be a likely candidate for homeschooling.

Stating that you need to like your children in order to succeed at homeschooling does not imply that someone who sends a child to school does not like her child. It also does not imply that you must find your child delightful to be with every moment of everyday. What I am saying is that when you homeschool, you will be in your child's company for many hours everyday. If you don't fundamentally enjoy your child's company, don't attempt to homeschool.

Children Learn What They Live

If children live with criticism,
They learn to condemn.
If children live with hostility,
They learn to fight.
If children live with ridicule,
They learn to be shy.
If children live with shame,
They learn to feel guilty.
If children live with encouragement,
They learn confidence.
If children live with tolerance,
They learn to be patient.
If children live with praise,
They learn to appreciate.
If children live with acceptance,
They learn to love.
If children live with approval,
They learn to like themselves.
If children live with honesty,
They learn truthfulness.
If children live with security,
They learn to have faith in themselves and others.
If children live with friendliness,
They learn the world is a nice place in which to live.

2. Have a sense of humor

Without a sense of humor being a mother can be a pretty grim business. As a homeschooling mother, humor becomes even more vital. There are days when life with young children just seems more than any one person can cope with. No matter how hard one tries, the more confused everything gets. Life with children around all the time can be stressful and hilarious. It depends on your point of view.

Laughter can be like a breath of fresh air in a stuffy room. Being able to laugh and see the humor in many situations helped me to deal with the complications and "busy-ness" of life with four children. Our family enjoys laughing together. We played games like Charades or Mad Libs that sometimes left us all laughing so hard we cried. We read books that made us laugh. As everyone grew older jokes gained popularity. Our humor is a gentle and positive kind, no sarcastic humor or teasing, just fun. We still continue to play Charades - either in pairs or each individual acting out a title of a book, movie, or song.

There are a number of books in print about the value of humor. There is even an organization called The Humor Project that puts on a Humor Conference to help people add more laughter to their lives. If you are interested in ideas about how to add positive humor to your life, write the Humor Project, 110 Spring St., Saratoga Springs, NY 12866 USA or check their web site for more information http://www.HumorProject.com/ .

3. Be able to read, write, and do basic math and be willing to upgrade skills as needed

You do not need a college or university degree to teach your child at home. You do need a basic proficiency in reading, writing, and math. If you can read children's picture books aloud, if you can write a letter, and if you can balance your checkbook, you have the basics I am talking about. Now don't panic about the checkbook balancing. Can you multiply, divide, and do addition and subtraction? Good enough.

As long as you can read, you can stay "one step ahead" of your children as you explore various areas of study by reading ahead on your own. You may feel that your understanding of some subjects is limited, and feel hesitant to attempt to teach these subjects. One thing to keep in mind is that one of the best ways to learn something is to teach it. My own understanding of things like the rotation of the planets around the sun increased immensely as I answered my children's questions.

You may find that what gave you trouble when you were 12 years old and in elementary school is not as difficult now. It can be quite a relief to look at a Grade 6 math book and find that the problems aren't as hard as they were when you were in Grade 6.

On the other hand if you look at the textbook and don't understand, then you may need to update your skills. There are often courses available for adults through community colleges and/or correspondence courses. One of the joys of taking courses as an adult is that the instructors on the whole are working hard to have you succeed. You are not a captive audience, you are a paying consumer of their services. This can be quite a refreshing feeling! You might also find that you can teach yourself what you need to know after asking someone you trust to explain how to start. There are many ways to acquire the knowledge necessary to teach your child.

I found that learning as an adult was not fraught with the tensions I had when learning in school as a child. Learning as an adult has been more relaxed because I made the decision to learn something. I was not forced. However, I have not taken any formal courses where grades were given. Most of the courses I have taken have been offered through volunteer training and have been informal classes set up so that everyone could learn and succeed.

4. Have a commitment to a philosophy that leads you to homeschool

I have a strong commitment to homeschooling. My philosophy developed from my experience as an aide in a grade 1 classroom in an inner city school when I was 20 years old. My first day on the job was quite a shock. I arrived early and was shown to the classroom where I had a chance to look around before school started and the children arrived. When the bell rang, there was no teacher! I was in quite a panic. I was in charge of the 26 six and seven-year-olds sitting at their desks, looking at me.

I didn't know what their routine was. I found no daily plan on the teacher's desk to help me. I had never been in a grade 1 classroom in the U.S. before, as I had lived in the Netherlands at that age. I can't remember exactly how I managed. I probably asked the children for their help so that I could follow their normal routine. After recess, one and a half hours later, the substitute teacher arrived. She took over for the rest of the day.

The school that hired me had a large grant from the Ford Foundation - making it possible to hire aides for each classroom. Money to purchase equipment, materials, and supplies were provided for as well. It looked like an ideal situation. Many people then, 1968, and now, thought that if schools only had adequate funding, all the problems that beset schooling would be solved.

From my first day on the job, I began to realize that while enough money could make school a more pleasant place to be, it could not solve all the problems that children have learning in school. During the next six months it became more and more clear to me that while school was a place where some children could learn, it was not necessarily the best place for all children to learn. For some children, it was a place where although they learned, they were not learning the three "Rs" - reading, writing and 'rithmetic. Instead, they learned about who they were in comparison to others. They learned that their parents' expectations and their teachers' expectations were sometimes in conflict. I found that what they were learning in the unrecognized curriculum of school culture jeopardized their faith in themselves and their ability to learn.

In order to understand more about children and what happened to them in school, I began to read a number of books about children in elementary schools. I had taken courses in early childhood education and child development at university. Now I wanted to know more about elementary education. Authors like John Holt (*How Children Learn* and *How Children Fail*) and Sylvia Ashton Warner (*Teacher*) provided me with much food for thought. It was at this time, working in a school that seemed to have everything a school could want, that I decided that if and when I had children they would not go to school. I would teach them at home for I was disheartened by what I saw.

The six months I spent working in an inner city school took place during a very impressionable time in my life. I enjoyed being with the children. I was fascinated to observe them working to master the art of reading. At the same time there was a sense of adventure in the school. A sense that the educators were trying new things to make a difference so that the children could succeed. The teacher and aide in the other grade 1 classroom were trying a method from England called Primary Integrated Schooling where children could choose what they wanted to work on from all the many materials available. There were few teacher led directives, just a creative environment.

All of this energy, all of these resources were directed toward improving education in inner city schools. It was exciting to be a part of all this. At the same time, I was aware of the tensions between parents and teachers. Most of the teachers were white, most of the aides were African American and 95% of the parents were African American. The teaching staff had a number of ideas about "whole language" type learning. The parents wanted their children to learn how to read, write, and to do math so that their children could succeed in life, and were uncertain about these new methods. The teachers felt that they knew better than the parents about the ways that children learn. The parents were not at all sure if they could trust the teachers and their ideas about how learning took place.

The students in my class varied in their ability to learn the material presented to them. Although many of them struggled to learn to read the grade 1 reader, all but two of them could read the graffiti painted on the walls in the neighborhood. I found myself questioning how sensible it was to place so many small children in a classroom with only two adults. I watched the interaction of the children in the class, the sorting that had been done by the children as to who was or was not acceptable. I wondered if all of this was necessary. I wondered too, about some of the children who were designated as having learning problems or behavioral problems. Was some of their behavior and lack of success in learning because they were not "bright" or was a classroom situation too stressful for them?

All these thoughts and observations rattled around in my head as I worked with these children. Thirty-one years later, I still think of these children - Tony (not his real name), who had a difficult time with the language arts tasks assigned to him. He was not yet ready to learn to read, but he loved listening to stories and singing. Then there was Patricia (not her real name) who had a difficult time grasping any information. Yet one day when playing with parquetry blocks, she made a most amazing symmetrical design that surprised and pleased both the teacher and me. We tried to find other ways to engage her in more learning activities but we could not find anything else that she could use to demonstrate her innate intelligence.

I wonder how their lives have turned out. Did the years in that school help them to be better able to cope in the world? I hope so. I hope that the care and the attention, the genuine desire to make school a better place to learn made a difference in their lives.

My next job was as a director of a daycare center. It became clear to me that here, as in schools, there was something askew with the way we value children in our society. The daycare was subsidized and provided employment for six staff. Most of the parents of the children who came to the center worked in the shoe factories in the area earning the minimum wage. They dropped their children off at 6:30 a.m. and picked them up 8 to 10 hours later. The 20 children in the center spent more time with the staff than with their parents. I worked there for about four months, a temporary director until they could find a permanent director. I was offered the job permanently, but I was unable to commit myself to something that felt so wrong. I could not accept that I had so much influence on these children's lives. I knew that if I accepted the job on a permanent basis my heart would break. I wanted to change the way child care was funded so that subsidies for child care went directly to the mothers. I wanted to find ways to help women learn the nurturing skills they needed to be able to be home with their children and enjoy them.

I know that those four months were good months for the children. They were also good months for me. I began cooking their lunches instead of buying them from a school lunch program. Whole foods gradually became a staple, no more Wonder bread! I baked bread for the center, the children helped and we had a good time. The janitor enjoyed the bread so much that he began to join us in the baking. Soon, he took over and started baking all the bread for us - half white/half whole wheat flour.

It was summer time, and we went swimming everyday. The children then returned to the center and had naps if they were under six or rested if they were over six. Most of them fell asleep because they had gotten up so early. When their parents came to pick them up, it was usually quiet. I made a point of being available with a plate of cookies and lemonade to let them know what their child had done that day. I asked the parents if they objected to the naps. "Did it make it harder for the children to go to sleep in the evening?" All of them said that although the children went to bed a little later, they were pleased to pick up children who were not tired and cranky. They appreciated the chance to talk with me and slow down a few minutes before going home to start supper.   My heart went out to each of them.

It seemed to me that these parents were caught in a bind (as are many parents today) that has no easy solution. Both daycare and school are places where, for good or ill, children are raised by people other than their parents. Children learn about attitudes, values, and ways of relating from their caretakers. This curriculum is unspoken and not acknowledged and has tremendous influence in children's lives.

I know that for many people, there are no alternatives to school and daycare. I know that for too many children, school and daycare is a safer place than home. And this both saddens me and makes me angry. I know that as a society we have the resources to make children's lives safe. We have the resources to support and encourage parents to learn to nurture their children. We just don't seem to be able to make the commitment to do so.

Many years passed before I had children. During those years, I was a nursery school teacher, swimming instructor and self-sufficient farmer. I enjoyed being with children. I had friends who homeschooled their children. I had many opportunities to talk with them about why they made the choice to keep their children at home instead of sending them to school. All of these experiences strengthened my earlier decision regarding schooling so that when my children were born, I knew that sending them to school would not be an option. Fortunately Larry, my husband and the father of my children, felt the same way.

Even though I felt so strongly about homeschooling, there were days when I had young children that I wanted nothing more than the peace and quiet that children attending school for part of the day would give me. I struggled to meet the various needs of my children and wondered if it was all worth while. As I struggled, I would remember why I made this decision and remember that the reasons I decided to homeschool still applied even though it involved hard work for me.

I believe that children learn best in an atmosphere where they are respected, loved and valued. I think it is important to encourage children to listen to their own inner voice. I think it is important that children have the opportunity to move at their own pace to master the skills needed to be competent in the world. I know that all children are inherently good and want to move toward mastering the skills they need in order to function. I believe that children need a structure in which to live, but a structure that is responsive to a child's cycles and takes them into account. I believe that children need adults around them who model integrity. I believe that children need adults who relate to them in respectful, caring ways so that a child can learn to relate in respectful and caring ways. I think that it is vital for a child to feel "safe" in his or her learning environment. At the same time, other people in the family also need to feel "safe." I feel strongly that given the opportunity and support needed, children will find their gifts.

I wouldn't have been able to formulate my philosophy as clearly when Josh was six years old. I can now define what I intuited to be true when I first started to homeschool my children. My philosophy has evolved through the experiences I have had living with my children. I imagine it will continue to evolve as my children grow older. That is one of the best things about being involved with children, there is always change and evolution.

Not all people are going to homeschool with the same philosophy. I have outlined the basics of my philosophy to clarify where I stand.   You may have a different philosophy that leads you to homeschool.   What I want to emphasize here is how important it is to have a strong commitment, a philosophy, to why you are homeschooling your children.   There are going to be many times when being a homeschooling mother will be a challenge.   Your commitment will help you to ground your frustrations and put them into the perspective of your long range goals.   (You may wish to use the information in the appendix on goal setting to help you define what your goals are in parenting and homeschooling your children.)

Having a philosophy behind your decision to homeschool also gives you direction.   If you homeschool only because you think the school system is terrible, then you are reacting to the school system.   This can give you the courage and strength to make a change in the beginning, but over time, a choice that is a reaction tends to cause more reactions.   I, personally, like to act rather than to re-act.   Re-acting can help us try something new, but it is just the opposite side of the coin from what we are re-acting to.   It is not a change, it is a flip, a swing of the pendulum from one side to the other.

Finding your own positive reasons to homeschool can help you to formulate your own homeschooling philosophy.   Your philosophy can then form a basis for your actions.   Actions are a way of going beyond the swinging pendulum to a new place.   When we act, we can have more freedom to choose the things we want to do based on their suitability rather than choosing to do something in reaction to its opposite.   It is a way of going between the two sides of the coin rather than going from one side to the other.

5. Be willing to develop communication/listening skills

Communication is the key to any relationship.   When your child was a baby, although he or she could not use words to express him/herself, you learned how to interpret and listen to his or her cues.   As your child grows older and more competent in making him/herself understood and begins to ask more complex questions, you will also need to develop your ability to communicate more clearly.   I thought that I was fairly adept at communicating.   I found to my dismay that I often confused my children with information that I thought was clear but the child found confusing.   I also found that my listening skills were not as good as I would have liked. I realized how often I talked rather than listened.

I think that listening is the key to effective parenting and home-schooling. Listening doesn't mean limiting yourself to the words a child is saying. It also means listening to the body language and underlying feelings of the child. This kind of listening is like the picking up of cues that one does with a small baby. Perhaps you can remember when your child was a baby. Before he or she would cry there was a series of cues he or she gave that let you know that crying was imminent. Cues continue beyond the baby years. The more in tune you are with your child's cues, the easier it is to understand and communicate with your child.

One of the most effective ways I've found to really listen to a child is to try to see things from a child's point of view, to remove my agenda from the situation. This often brings me a fresh perspective.

6. Be prepared to receive criticism for your decision to homeschool.

For many homeschoolers, the decision to homeschool is one that causes great upheavals and concern among extended family members. Grandparents, aunts, uncles, brothers, sisters, etc. all feel like they must say something and express their concern that you have made this choice. Homeschooling your child is a parenting decision that can affect the extended members of your family because it is so visible.

For example, grandparents may find that their friends ask "How is your grandchild doing in school?" If they are uncomfortable answering this question, they will more than likely pass on their discomfort to you as a criticism of your choice to homeschool.

It might be helpful to prepare your extended family by letting them know why you have made the decision to homeschool. When you give them this information, let them know you are not expecting to persuade them one way or the other, you are just informing them. Giving extended family members information about why you are homeschooling and not expecting agreement may ease tensions. Impart this information to family members when no children are present. Make it clear to extended family members that if they have concerns about homeschooling, the concerns need to be expressed to you not to your child or children.

All of this sounds very calm, logical and reasonable, and I wish I could have been calm, logical and reasonable each time someone questioned my choices. Fortunately, I had already made so many different choices before having children that my choice to homeschool did not surprise my extended family. I received very little criticism for our choice to homeschool from extended family members. The criticism I received in the early years came from friends and acquaintances. This was at times quite devastating, yet when I weighed the criticism against my inner convictions, I saw that it was my desire to be liked by everyone that was threatened by people's criticism. Being liked by everyone has never been my goal.

When someone questions my decision regarding homeschooling, I find that it's more helpful if I discuss the positive aspects of homeschooling rather than the negatives of school. The positive reasons are often easier for someone to accept. Some people are threatened by my choice to homeschool and feel that it is a criticism of their choices of education for their children. When I state the reasons for my choices in positive terms based on my feelings and perceptions, then, although the people I'm speaking with may disagree, it is often easier for them to accept my choice.

I remember an exchange I had with a teacher who could not understand why I would not want to put my children in her class. I asked her if she enjoyed her job. She said she did. I asked her if she enjoyed helping children learn to read. She did. I told her that I enjoyed that, too. I liked being a part of the process of my child learning to read or learning other things about the world. I enjoyed being able to observe the insights that my children had as they connect one thing with another. She seemed more relaxed after that conversation. My reasons for homeschooling were not against her or other members of the teaching profession. My reasons were personal and positive, similar to her reasons for choosing to be a teacher.

If withstanding criticism for your choice to homeschool is a bit scary for you, you might want to consider taking a course in self-esteem, assertiveness, and/or communication skills. Part of maturing is accepting that some of the choices you make about how you live your life may offend others. This happens to everyone. Homeschooling can be a way to find strengths you weren't aware of as you find ways to stay true to your own beliefs while at the same time accepting that others may not agree with you. As my children have grown older, I don't feel as vulnerable. I also have "proof of the pudding." My children are capable, self-motivated learners, able to listen and converse with others, "coachable," and delightful people to be around.

7. Have a support system or network and/or a supportive partner.

One of the main criticisms I heard when Josh was about 6 years old was that I was being too overprotective and had my children tied to my apron strings. This kind of comment would disturb my equilibrium for quite awhile when I had young children. I felt so defensive, so vulnerable. I found it essential to have other women to talk to who, while they might not have made the decision to homeschool, did choose to have close relationships with their children. I joined a group that supported me in my choice of mothering my children. This contact with other women who were also exploring what it meant to have close, loving relationships with their children helped me to feel less isolated.

La Leche League was my support group for many years. Although as an organization it is dedicated to helping mothers breastfeed their babies, it is also a group that supports mothers in meeting the needs of their babies and children - a unique thing in our North American culture that focuses more on adult needs than on children's needs.

I learned from a friend in La Leche League to laugh when someone suggested that I had my children tied to my apron strings. Her response was always "You're darn right. And I've got them tied good and tight, too." I found that agreeing with someone often took the wind out of his or her sails, broke the tension, and allowed the conversation to move on.

Your support system can be for homeschooling and/or for mothering. It doesn't need to be big - a few close friends can make a big difference if they are able to listen and support you in your choices.

In many places there are meetings for homeschoolers where home-schooling issues are discussed. Some people find these helpful. If you try one homeschooling support group and it doesn't quite suit you, try another one. Others prefer sympathetic friends who may not have made a comparable decision but are willing to offer a listening ear and support. On-line support groups for homeschooling have proliferated in the two years since the first edition of this book was published. Many people find these virtual communities very helpful.

Do some exploring and see what you can find in your community. If you live in a rural area and can't find anyone close by, check your library for information about homeschooling networks. Reaching out to others helps you to feel less isolated. Talking with other women about homeschooling or other mothering concerns can give you a different perspective on your situation.

La Leche League succeeds because it is a place where women share their stories. Mothers of very young babies hear the stories of mothers whose babies are slightly older. Sharing the struggles, problems, challenges, and joys of mothering allows all the mothers at these meetings to put their personal experience in a context and see their lives as part of a bigger picture. Sharing your concerns and worries about homeschooling with someone who has lived through some similar worries can help you feel more comfortable and may help you find solutions that hadn't occurred to you. Each child is different. Each family is different, yet we all have common themes of concern. Having a place to air those concerns can help you find your own unique way to address that concern and find what works best for you. That's one of the best things about homeschooling - each family finds unique ways to homeschool. There are probably as many ways to homeschool as there are people who do it.

One of the benefits of homeschooling is having time to form a network of supportive friends. You have time to form deep and valuable friendships with other like-minded women that you might not have had time for if you were doing some other kind of work. Your children can play together and you can share ideas, worries, things that worked, things that didn't work, help each other figure out why something didn't work as well as explore new ideas.

Be sure that the support group you have is actually supportive. In other words, air your grievances about homeschooling only to those who have no vested interest in you changing your method of education. If your mother is quite concerned about you not sending your daughter to school, she would not be a good person to talk to when you feel that you are at the end of your rope with your daughter. Even if the thing that is driving you crazy might be typical behavior for an 8 year old girl, your mother may tell you that "If only you sent her to school, this would not be a problem."

When we choose to raise our children in ways that are different from the culture around us, then whatever behavior a child shows that might be irritating to his elders is usually attributed to whatever we are doing that is different from the dominant culture. It happens that way for women who nurse their babies. "The baby is doing this because you nurse him all the time" is a comment many mothers have heard from a critical relative when whatever the baby is doing is normal baby behavior but not a behavior that this person approves of or likes. It is so easy for someone who disapproves of your decision to homeschool to attribute any behavior of your child that you find hard to cope with a result of homeschooling. When you are struggling to understand a child's behavior, this way of attributing the behavior to your choice to homeschool is not supportive.

Many times, as I struggled to understand my child's behavior I wondered whether:
- the behavior was due to the fact that this child was being homeschooled
- it was typical for the age or
- due to factors I did not even know about.

If you find that those you turn to for support are suggesting that your problems could be easily solved by changing your method of education, you might want to find another support person who can allow you to think things through without having a ready-made solution for your problems.

Learning about child development can also provide support for your own perceptions and observations of your children. Libraries are a good source of books about children's development. Books about or by Jean Piaget on his theories of early childhood development are a good place to start. Keep in mind that some of what is considered normal child development for children of school age and beyond may be school induced development and not necessarily a natural part of child development.

School culture is so dominant that those who do research in the field of child development are often not aware of the influence of school culture. They describe some of children's developmental behavior as human development when in actuality it is developmental behavior taking place in the context of going to school. Those who study child development are becoming aware of the importance of taking into consideration cultural bias when studying children in different parts of the world. It will take time for people to realize that school is a culture as well and that it influences a child's development.

A book that I found interesting and informative regarding children's development is *Your Child's Growing Mind: A Guide to Learning and Brain Development from Birth to Adolescence* by Jane M. Healy, Ph.D. This book is a compilation of the most current theories on nervous system development and how this information applies to how children learn. I found it confirmed my own observation of my children. The author has also written a book that addresses schooling and the need for change within schools that seems to me to speak eloquently on behalf of homeschooling. (The author tried to teach her child at home and found it did not work for her. She draws the conclusion from her one experience that teaching a child at home will not work for anyone else either. Her conclusion about homeschooling clearly illustrates how important it is to avoid making blanket statements.)

Even with this author's blind spot about homeschooling, I found the information about cognitive development in her book fascinating. The information in the book can be used as a gauge to determine how realistic your expectations for certain learning tasks are for a child of a particular age.

Learning more about child development can help you deal with criticism as well as help you to be a better homeschooling mother. If you can state that "Studies show that children of this age vary in their ability to do math," your critic hears that you are knowledgeable. People usually express criticism out of their concern. Grandmas and grandpas want their grandchildren to have the best chance to do well in life. Homeschooling may be difficult for them to accept because it is so different from what they did as parents.

Using empathetic listening skills when someone is criticizing your choice of education is an option that may also be helpful. Empathetic listening is a way of listening for the feeling in the words that someone is expressing, i.e., "What do you mean you're not sending her to school? How will she ever be able to cope in the world and get a job?" Empathetic response "When you think about her future you're worried that she won't be able to make it." As an empathetic listener, you don't take what the speaker is saying personally, as something you need to defend, fix, or explain. Instead, you respond with empathy and concern for the speaker's feelings.

There are a number of books that have been written about this kind of listening: *People Skills* by Robert Bolton and *How To Talk So Kids Will Listen and Listen So Kids Will Talk* by Adele Faber and Elaine Mazlish are two that I have found particularly helpful. It is amazing how often people are really looking for an empathetic response rather than any other kind.

When your empathy is genuine, it means that you are listening and walking in that other person's shoes. You are not trying to either defend your point of view or change the other person's point of view. It is a very useful communication tool. Learning empathetic listening skills is like learning a new language. It takes practice to acquire the skills needed to do it well. It is worth taking time to become proficient in this new language. It will help your communication with your children as well as with those who may criticize you.

If you have a partner/husband, homeschooling will be less draining for you if you and your partner agree to homeschool. Two people may agree to homeschool and yet have two entirely different ideas of what this means. It is important for you and your partner to talk about expectations for the children and the issues involved such

as:
1. who is responsible for what
2. is this an experiment and does it have a time limit
3. what are the criteria we will use to judge if this is working
4. will we do school at home, child-led learning, etc.

Discussing these issues enable you to see where you agree and where you may disagree about homeschooling. It will take time to resolve any differences. How well you can work together even when you disagree depends on your commitment both to the idea of homeschooling and your relationship. Each couple works this out over time.   The goal would be to find a way that you can support each other as you homeschool your children.

Homeschooling can be a strain on a marriage. It more than likely means one income, or the equivalent of one income as someone needs to be with the child (children) all the time. It means that there will be child oriented activities all through the day and into the evening, as well as children's toys and materials being a more prevalent part of the household. It may mean that mom needs time to herself and only gets it at night when the children are in bed asleep. There may be less couple time. I am not trying to discourage anyone from homeschooling. I am trying to give you a realistic picture of the stresses and strains of having children around 24 hours a day.

I know women who have homeschooled although their partners have not been 100% supportive. Their commitment to provide a learning environment suited to their children's needs was so strong that they were willing to risk their relationship with their partner. I feel blessed that my husband and I have agreed about the "hows" of homeschooling. He has given me lots of reassurance as well as support. He is an elementary school teacher, teaching grade 4/5. He has been a great resource both for materials and maintaining a perspective. I can not imagine how it would have been to homeschool without his support, encouragement, and involvement.

This does not mean that we did not have struggles. We did, many of them! However, these struggles have more to do with the struggles that most couples face when they have children and live together - issues about emotions, housework, sex, time, and space.

On the issue of homeschooling, we have been in accord. Because we saw eye to eye on the issues of homeschooling, we have learned to work together on other issues.

Stages of learning

We all come to a new venture with a great deal of hope and many expectations about how it's going to work. I found it helpful to know that people seem to acquire the ability to do thing in stages. Let me use the example that Kathleen Auerbach, RN and Lactation Consultant, used when she presented this idea at a La Leche League Conference. She was speaking about how mothers acquire the ability to mother. She used an example from her own early months as a mother.

In the first stage of learning, we think there is only one way to do something. A diaper salesman came to Kathleen's house when she was pregnant with her first child and showed her how to fold a diaper. She had not folded diapers before, so she assumed that "This is the way to fold diapers." After her baby was born, she always folded his diapers precisely the way she had been shown by that diaper salesman.

In the second stage of learning, we begin to experiment. Kathleen found that every once in a while she didn't manage to fold the diaper exactly as shown and nothing terrible happened. The diaper still fulfilled it's function.

The third stage of learning is the mastery stage where we see that we can make of this situation what we like based on our own observations and experience. Kathleen realized that as long as the diaper was attached to her baby, it would serve it's function. How it was folded was not as vital as she once thought.

Reviewing that process of acquiring a new skill:
Stage 1 - Beginning Stage
There's only one way to do something.
Stage 2 - Experimentation Stage
Let's see if this will work if I try this another way.
Stage 3 - Mastery Stage
I have incorporated my own experience to do this my way.

Each of us goes through similar stages as we acquire new information and learn. One of the most challenging things about working with children is that just when we feel that we have mastered how to mother a 2 month old, a child grows and changes. We must start again and go through these stages to learn how to mother a 6 month old, etc.

When we start to homeschool, we have a picture of how it is going to be and how it will work. I remember when Josh was 3½ years old. I was having a very difficult time. I wasn't getting the response from him that I expected. I had been a nursery school teacher. I thought I should be an expert with this age. I remembered mothers of the students in my nursery school marveling at how patient I was with their children and how responsive their children were to me. I found, much to my chagrin, that now that I was a mother I had very little patience. I felt concern for Josh because I ran out of patience so often.

I spoke with my husband at length one evening and shared my worries and concerns. I suggested that contrary to my strong stand on homeschooling we should send Josh to nursery school. There he would have people around him who weren't always being frustrated with him. During our discussion, something shifted for me. I realized that I was holding so tightly to the idea of what a 3½ year old should be like and what a mother of a 3½ year old should be like, that I couldn't see Josh for who he was. I managed to let go of the strangle hold my ideas had on my ability to respond to my child. My perception shifted. Whatever had been driving me over the edge no longer had that power.

I was grateful that my husband could listen to me in such a supportive way even though he felt very strongly about the importance of homeschooling. He helped me to find a solution to my dilemma that didn't involve another dilemma, conflicting belief systems. He helped me to work through the various stages of learning by just listening to me and allowing me to express my emotions about the situation. This enabled me to see that my picture of being the mother of a 3½ year old and having a 3½ year old was like having to fold the diaper a certain way - it wasn't quite that rigid. I could find my own way by responding to my child instead of trying to fit him into my preconceived ideas.

8. Be able to learn from mistakes

My children know that making mistakes is a natural part of learning. They are not afraid to make mistakes when they try something new. They know that there are many ways to go about solving a problem and that not every problem has one "right" answer.

A baby learning to walk makes many "mistakes" and falls down. Eventually, through trial and error, persistence, and practice, the baby learns to walk. Each "mistake" helped the child to learn that "no, this doesn't work, I have to try a slightly different way of balancing to stay moving and upright." The difficult thing for me to accept is that while I was learning how to be a mother, I made mistakes on my children. I can get quite carried away by the mistakes I made and focus exclusively on those things I wish I had not done. I can't seem to let go of them. I read something in *Mastering Your Hidden Self* by Serge King that has helped me to learn to accept my mistakes and learn from them.

> "Repentance, which may include atonement, has been greatly misunderstood. It is almost always interpreted as meaning 'to feel sorry or miserable about what you have done.' That doesn't do you or anyone else any good. What repentance really means is to change your way of thinking and to act differently. Just to feel sorry is meaningless; you have to do something about it. That something may be an attitude you can change or an act you can perform quite on your own, or it may have to involve someone else, in which case it is called 'atonement.'

> "Now atonement is another word that has been greatly misunderstood. It is usually taken to mean that you have to 'pay back' a person or society or even God for something you did wrong, and this paying back can be in the form of money, a good deed, or the undergoing of punishment. All of this is a distortion. Atonement actually means 'to become reconciled' (i.e., 'friendly again,' from the Middle English 'at one', 'in accord') or 'to make amends.' The latter term, 'amends,' means 'to improve one's conduct,' not to make up

for something or to pay something (c.f. Webster's).

"The third step in forgiveness, absolution (the same thing as pardon) comes from a Latin word meaning 'to set free,' and is essentially a declaration that one is set free from guilt, blame or obligation.

"In practical terms to forgive yourself, you acknowledge your mistakes, change your ways, and make the decision to pardon yourself. Of course it is nice if someone else pardons you, but that won't have any effect unless you accept it, so it all comes down to pardoning yourself. If feeling guilty is habitual, even if you have changed your ways, then you will have to replace it with the habit of feeling pardoned. If you have the belief that you should be punished, then you must either eliminate the 'should' idea from your consciousness or find a way to punish yourself once that will be effective in convincing your ku (subconscious) that it's enough while not being too harmful." (from page 93. See page 34 of *Mastering Your Hidden Self* for a more complete definition of Ku.)

I find this approach helps me when I get depressed about some of the things I did when my children were younger. It helps me to know that changing my behavior is repentance. It helps me to remember that in order for me to model that it is OK to make mistakes, I need to be gentle with myself when I make them.

Being able to accept my own mistakes leads me to look at the judgments I have made about myself. Do I, deep down inside myself, really believe that I am a "good" person or do I believe that I am "bad?" Depending on my I answer, I can give myself permission to not know something or to not understand something, or I can look at my mistake as proof that I am "bad."

You may wonder what this has to do with homeschooling. Why is it important to look at the way you treat yourself when you make a mistake? If you are homeschooling your children, your attitude toward mistakes becomes the atmosphere in which your children learn. That is why I think it is important to look at this issue. Alice Miller, in her later books *Banished Knowledge* and *Breaking the Wall of Silence* discusses how difficult it is for us as adults to deal in a positive way with mistakes because accepting mistakes, acknowledging them, means facing our own unresolved pain as children when people/parents blamed us for the mistakes we made.

When my two older boys were little, I would sometimes think that their actions, which were typical for their age, were motivated by intentions of wanting to hurt or cause pain. In other words, I sometimes assumed that their intentions were "bad." When I would take the time to think about this and look underneath my assumptions of their behavior, I knew that my children weren't "bad." How could they be, they did not have the depth of experience needed to act with any "bad" intent.

But in the heat of two little boys fighting with each other, I would loose my rational perspective. It has taken me years of thinking this through, and observing my children to see how often I infer a motive for an action that says more about myself than about my child. This thinking and observing is part of the work Alice Miller talks about in her books.

A six year old who is being bothered might throw something at the person who's bothering him. Throwing things at people (except as part of playing some sort of game like baseball, basketball, etc.) is not acceptable behavior in our house. When this happened, I would intervene and help my child learn a more acceptable way to express his anger and frustration at being bothered. However, the behavior does not mean that the child is "bad."

I read about this idea (a child's behavior is not necessarily a reflection of his/her character) many times in many books about parenting. I read again and again that a child needs to be shown how to express anger, rage, and frustration appropriately. It took me many hours of thought to discover how to really apply this truth when mothering my children. What helped me to work through this was constantly referring to my belief that all children are inherently "good." I had to go through the three stages of learning that I described earlier many times before I finally got it.

Assigning inappropriate motives to children's behavior is part and parcel of the pedagogy of child-rearing in our Western patriarchal belief system. Let me illustrate with an example from when Josh was a toddler under 2 years old. At that time, Josh had a desperate desire to communicate with words and had such a difficult time pronouncing the words he wanted to use. Someone who observed Josh at this time commented to me that this difficulty was a sign of his laziness and my over-responsiveness to him. Josh didn't talk because he didn't need to talk. I responded to him even though he wasn't talking clearly. I was rendered speechless by this comment! It was so obvious to me that the person who said this had not observed Josh very closely. He would sometimes be in tears because I couldn't quite interpret what he wanted to say. He tried so hard to communicate and be understood!

The philosophy that this view represents - that children are lazy and must be made to learn - is very strong in our North American society. Even though I consciously do not believe this is true, I sometimes catch myself operating as though it were true. When this happens, I remind myself that a child wants to gain competency and wants to be able to function in the world. Blaming a child for making mistakes and labeling him as lazy is not conducive to learning.

Many children do not follow the time table for learning or competency that adults have in mind. When this happens, adults will frequently begin to make assumptions about why a child is not learning certain things, as in the example above. This can lead to all sorts of incriminations and assumptions about a child's motives that can lead to a child refusing to learn anything at all in order to maintain his sense of control over himself.

As my children have made mistakes in the process of learning to read and do math, I would remind myself of the necessity of making mistakes. A child is not deliberately driving an adult crazy when she doesn't understand something. A different approach needs to be found so that the child can grasp the ideas presented.

Let me illustrate this point with an incident that my brother remembers from his first weeks in kindergarten. Our family moved from the Netherlands to the U.S. in 1956. My brother was 5 years old at the time. About three weeks after our arrival, he started kindergarten. He didn't speak English, so he didn't understand the kindergarten teacher when she spoke to him. He remembers that she would start to yell at him because he could not understand. She would get louder and louder and more and more angry, implying that he was "dumb" because he didn't understand her. He remembers wondering what was wrong with her. Why couldn't she speak to him in Dutch? He could communicate just fine with his sisters and parents.

We often get louder and angrier when a child does not understand. Perhaps just as my brother did not understand the language the teacher was speaking, our children don't understand our language and we need to find a way to communicate in their language. We need to trust in their ability to achieve mastery and allow them to make mistakes and learn from those mistakes just as they did when they were learning to walk. We also need to trust in our own development and learn from the mistakes we make.

9. Be willing to develop limit-setting skills

As a mother, it is essential to acquire the ability to set limits and/or define boundaries. As a homeschooling mother, this skill is even more vital. I once heard someone say to me about a homeschooled child "No wonder that child doesn't go to school. He is totally unruly and disruptive. Nobody would let him stay in school." This surprised me as I had not equated unruly children and homeschooling. After hearing this comment I began to think of how homeschooling could lead to unruly children. I realized that in making the decision to homeschool, many parents are searching for a more free-flowing form of education with no adult imposed learning agenda. Because there is a swing away from an adult imposed learning agenda, any form of adult expectations is also discarded and there are no guidelines for behavior. This leads to chaos and an overwhelmed family.

While I believe strongly that children need to have room to learn at their own rate, children also need to live within expectations of responsible and caring behavior. In other words, while I do not expect my children to master reading by a certain age, I do expect them to behave in such a way that makes it safe for everyone in our household - no hitting, biting, throwing, etc. While this standard of behavior is expected, I am also aware that a child may be able to understand something (like no hitting) long before she or he may be able to act on it. In the face of angry feelings, my children needed help to be able follow our family rules.

To set limits and family rules, you need to respect your children and yourself - to feel as though you are worthy of being treated with kindness and consideration. In other words, you can treat your children with respect and still have children who are unaware of other's needs and requirements, if you do not also teach your child to treat you and others with respect. This word "respect" can have such negative connotations that I want to demonstrate what I mean with an example.

When a small child climbs on mom's lap and sits there, he sometimes hurts his mom by kicking and/or pinching as he climbs up or bumping up and down on her lap once he gets there. This behavior is not intended to hurt. The small child is unaware of the effect his actions have. To begin to teach a child to show respect for you, his mother, it is important for you to let the child know that this hurts. You might say something like, "When you climb up on me this way, it hurts me. If you want to get up on my lap, just tell me and I will pick you up." You show your child affection at the same time that you are setting a limit - Mommy is not for hurting.

The next time your small child begins to climb up on your lap and it hurts, you stop him, remove him from the climbing position he's in, lift him up on your leg, and say again, "It hurts me when you climb up on me like that. Mommies are not for hurting." You may need to have this conversation a hundred times, a thousand times. Each time you have this interchange you stick to your limit and respond to your child's need to sit in your lap. If you can anticipate when the climbing is going to happen, then that's all the better. You have sidestepped one of the steps and progressed to a new step by lifting your child as soon as he looks like he would like to be on your lap.

If a child persists in hurting, it is time to look at how you give attention to your child. Does your child only receive attention when he hurts you? Give him your positive attention by playing with him. Go outside and run about or read a story together, lifting your child up into your lap or something else that gives your child your focused attention. This stops the need to get attention by hurting you. The reason hurting works is because we respond. A child learns quickly just what will make his mother respond to him.

The book *Don't Shoot The Dog* by Karen Prior has very helpful information about positive reinforcement and how to use it effectively. The author is an animal trainer and draws on her experience to explain how to use positive reinforcement effectively. She mentions in this book that among animal trainers there is a suggestion that people not be allowed to have children until they can teach a chicken to dance. That always gave me food for thought.

I used a young child for my example of how to set a limit because it is when children are young that we begin to demonstrate how to treat others with respect and courtesy. As you meet your child's need for attention and your physical presence, you make it clear when something hurts or is uncomfortable for you with actions as well as words. If you do not let your child know when something he is doing hurts, you are doing your child a disservice.

Small children need physical contact with their parents. They are not aware that their actions can be hurtful. They need guidance to show them how they can have this close physical contact so that it is pleasant for both the child and the parent. You define what is acceptable behavior for your child (Mommies are not for hurting) and you help your child learn this behavior by lovingly reminding him when necessary with both your actions and your words.

For small children in particular it is your actions - picking up your child as he starts to climb up on your lap or helping him climb up so that it doesn't hurt - that is important. Words are not enough. You need to show your child what you mean. This establishes clear and effective communication. You are not asking your children to read your mind or interpret your body language. You set limits that define for your child how to climb or sit on your lap.

Young children who have had limits established for them in an atmosphere of love and respect grow into older children who are comfortable with reasonable limits. Let me give you an example: Robin (who was 12 years old at the time) and his friend, Robert, (almost 12 years old) were riding their bikes through an obstacle course they had set up in our back yard. I was getting ready to take my older boys to the golf course. I had a number of things I needed to do before I could go. I asked Josh to tell them that I needed them to stop riding their bikes while I was gone and come in the house and have some lunch. The two boys readily agreed to this. They could see the sense of not engaging in such a challenging big muscle activity when they were home by themselves. I was gone about 30 minutes. As soon as I came back the boys went out again and started riding.

Limit setting involves thinking ahead to how a child might respond in a certain situation and being prepared. The old adage "An ounce of prevention is worth a pound of cure" could have been thought of just for mothers. Limit setting means defining what is not acceptable behavior, saying "no," it also means defining what is acceptable behavior, saying "yes."

Let me give you an another example. I took my daughter, Holly, with me to a couple of weekend long meetings when she was 5 and 6 years old. Before going, we talked about what she could expect - that I would be talking and listening in meetings. We needed to think about the things she could bring so that she could play quietly. She could climb into my lap and do things sitting in my lap, but I would not be able to read to her during the meetings. I explained that during my breaks I would read or do things just with her and that we would go to the zoo together before the meetings started.

Holly thought she could do this. She looked forward to the trip to the zoo because she was interested in animals. I knew she could manage during the meetings because she had entertained herself at other shorter meetings.

We flew on an airplane, arrived early, went to the zoo and were ready for the meetings when they started. She was the only child present and managed quite well. She had my physical presence even though she did not have my undivided attention. She climbed into my lap to draw pictures or play with playdough when she needed to.   We talked briefly at various times when she needed help with things.   During my breaks, she had my attention. We went swimming, read a story, or did something that she wanted to do. We had a good time together. The other adults were delighted by her presence. We still talk of those weekends. She understood what was expected of her before we left because we talked about it at length before hand. I showed her the limits of the situation and prepared us both by talking about what she could expect. We planned together what toys she wanted to bring.

My daughter was not ready to be separated from me for a whole weekend at that time. I wasn't ready for that either, knowing how much she still needed my sheer physical presence. I knew that she would be able to entertain herself as long as we brought the right toys; I made sure to spend some focused time with her throughout each day; and we spent time together at night.

Although she didn't have my attention as much as she would have liked, she did have my presence. She was also old enough to see that although it was tiresome to be in the meetings, we did some special things both before and after the meetings like going to the zoo or swimming in the hotel pool. She was able to accept the limits of the situation. Had she not been able to do this, I would have chosen not to go because neither one of us was ready for that long a period of separation.

A year later, when Noah (who was almost 14 years old at the time) was diagnosed as having diabetes, I stayed with him in the hospital for 11 days. My husband stayed home from work and brought Holly to the hospital everyday. She was 7 years old and understood how much Noah needed me. She expressed her anguish about not being with me in tears, especially when leaving to go home. She also told me that when she was home it wasn't as bad as when she was saying good-bye to me at the hospital. She was able to express and deal with the mixture of feelings she had. I was able to listen to her feelings and not discredit them.

As my children learned to live within the limits I set on their behavior, they also learned that I listened to them, to their need to be heard and considered. That is what respect is all about. *Webster's II New Riverside Dictionary* definition of respect "To feel or show deferential regard for: esteem." I cannot teach my child about self-respect or self-esteem without also teaching him to hold others in esteem - to be respectful of others.

While I expect my children to treat others with the same consideration and courtesy with which they would like to be treated, I also accept that they are children and will make mistakes. I am still learning (motherhood provides many opportunities to learn) and

I'm a lot older than they are. It takes practice to do anything well. Living in a family and homeschooling offers a great opportunity to practice showing care and consideration for oneself and others.

Many questions of "who gets to do what when" come up when you have more than one person living in a household. Sorting out family values and philosophy is something that all parents do. As a homeschooling mother, you spend more time with your children, so more situations will come up that require you to define the family's values and philosophy. It can be quite challenging! At the same time, one of the greatest benefits of homeschooling is that you can form your family's values and philosophy without the constant bombardment of contrasting values that school often presents to many children. One of the concerns I have heard parents express when their child starts school at age 5, is the difficulty their child has sorting out the different expectations and values school presents.

For example, when a child at home wants to ask a question, he finds a parent and asks. At school, he must raise his hand and be recognized by his teacher before asking his question. The teacher will only recognize the child at certain times. Sometimes, children are discouraged from asking questions because it disrupts the flow of what the teacher is doing, or age peers may tease a child about his questions. A child who has been encouraged to be curious and has had his questions seriously considered and answered might find the teacher's and his age peers' response to his questions confusing. Over time, a child adjusts and learns when to ask questions and, depending on how vulnerable he is to his age peers, whether he asks questions at all. Homeschooling offers the opportunity to limit the conflicting values a young child faces.

This does not mean that there won't ever be any conflicting values for a homeschooled child. I can remember a baseball coach suggesting to me that my sons needed to be more aggressive when playing ball. If there was someone in the way on the base path, they should just learn to run him down. My boys were not interested in running someone down to improve their baseball skills. The coach thought that it made good baseball sense to do this. My sons disagreed. They didn't think that risking injury made good baseball sense, nor did it suit their personal style.

In setting limits for children, you also model how they can set limits for themselves - an important skill to have. It is OK to say "no" to your child. You will also have your child saying "no" to you. Although we may at times want instant compliance from a child, we need to be aware of how important it is for a child to be able to say "no" to an adult. If we want our children to be able to listen to their own inner voice, we have to expect that there will be conflict between what we want a child to do and what that child wants to do. Listening and negotiating are all part of the skills you practice as a mother. As a homeschooling mother, you'll have even more opportunities to practice this skill. At the same time, because you will be spending more time with your children and have less random outside influence, you may find that after the initial hard work of defining family rules, you will have more time to enjoy the benefits of your children's respect and consideration for themselves, each other, and you as they grow older.

10. Be willing to develop patience

Many people say to me, "Oh, I could never teach my children. I don't have the patience." They comment on my patience and assume that this is a quality that I was born with. Certainly, if you don't have any interest in learning patience, homeschooling your children would not be a good idea. However, if you are willing to **develop** patience, homeschooling provides many opportunities to do so.

I found breathing to be one of the best things to do when I had exhausted my patience. Over time, I have developed ways to be patient. Patience doesn't mean being a martyr. It means being willing to give things time, including yourself. When I run out of patience, I try to change what I am doing rather than losing my temper. I try to be aware of when my patience is real and when it is not.

When my two older boys were younger, they excelled at detecting when my patience was a pretended patience. You know the kind – it oozes insincerity. They made it very clear to me that if I was just using a technique rather than really listening, it wasn't going to work. I learned to admit when I don't have patience for something and ask for cooperation rather than pretending to be patient.

For instance, when I am writing, I will let all of my children know that I need to concentrate and have very little patience for being interrupted for the next hour.   This is part of limit setting, letting people who live with you know what they can expect from you.

When my children were young, I liked using the expression used in *How To Talk So Kids Will Listen And Listen So Kids Will Talk* to describe my patience - "It's as big as a watermelon," or "It's as small as a pea and shrinking."   When I am rushed because I have been on the run all day my patience is "as small as a pea."   This is not the time I invite anyone into the kitchen to help me make a meal.

When my children were younger and were cooking or baking, I sometimes left the kitchen because all I saw was the mess being made rather than the food that was being created.   Unless I can be present with patience, I don't start an activity with my children that requires presence and   patience.   Of course there have been and continue to be many times when my children required my presence and patience and I had to find the patience required.   Breathing and looking into their eyes helped.

I am sure that most of us carry an image around in our heads of "the perfect mother."   Mine is someone who never loses her temper, makes cookies with her children and doesn't get frustrated by the mess, keeps the house spotless, reads and plays games with her children, is always available, never wants time to herself, and has oodles of patience.   Part of my learning patience has consisted of my tackling this impossible model I carry around with me.   I lose patience with myself for not being this "perfect" woman.   Humor often restores my perspective.   So does breathing.   I find it helpful to breathe deeply three or four times when I am at the edge, and during that time to imagine myself a tree with roots growing down deep into the ground, and sunlight coming through my leaves.

Breastfeeding my children helped me to learn to do this slowing down.   One of the great gifts that breastfeeding provides a mother is that as you nurse you need to sit.   As the baby nurses, a hormone (prolactin) is released that has a calming affect.   I learned, while nursing each of my four children, how important it was to slow down and look them in the eyes and be reminded of just what mothering is all about.   When I look one of my children in the eyes, I am refreshed by the love that we share, I become reconnected to my child, and my patience is often restored. I find that there is a shift in my perception.

Since my last baby weaned, I have had to consciously decide to relax instead of relying on a hormone to do it for me. I am glad I had as many years of nursing babies/toddlers as I did, so that I could learn how effective this slowing down is for my ability to be patient and keep things in perspective.

It is so easy to get caught up and move at a fast nonstop pace. However, sometimes slowing down, slowing the pace inside ourselves gives us more room to maneuver.   Let me give you an example. When Josh plays the harp, he is often playing notes in very rapid succession. He never looks hurried, his hands stay relaxed and he takes all the time allotted to play the notes. There is no sense of hurry even when he is moving rapidly. Instead, there is a sense of grace, of being in the present. I try to keep this in mind as I drive Holly to her dance lessons and we are a little late. My being in a rush inside my head isn't going to get us there any faster.

11. Be willing to develop observational skills

In order to help a child learn something, it is vital that you know the child. The difference for me between teaching my children at home and teaching in a school setting is that I have the opportunity to observe my children. Teachers in school settings also learn about children by observation, but very few of them have the opportunity for the almost unlimited time and access that a homeschooling mother can have. In the process of observing my children, I have learned how differently they all acquire knowledge. What works for one child has not necessarily worked for another.

When they were younger, I played with them with blocks, Lego, dolls, cars and trucks, puzzles, etc. This play time helped me to see how they processed information. I used opportunities as they arose to present a new idea to a child or to suggest a different approach to accomplish whatever was being played with. The years I spent observing my children helped me to be sensitive to their own particular learning styles. I found it fascinating to note their differences and similarities.

As I worked with my children on something like reading, I continually monitored their feelings. If they were having fun and enjoying themselves, we continued. If they were barely tolerant, we set a time limit and stuck to it. I sometimes said, "It looks to me as though you are really enjoying this." I made my observations available to them. They gave me feedback as well by telling me about their feelings and perceptions as we worked together. In this way, I modeled the importance of observation, of being in touch with oneself, while doing something.

One of the ways we learn about how the world functions is by observing and drawing conclusions and then testing them - a scientific approach to life. The greater our ability to observe, to increase our vision, the wider our understanding can be. Observing my children has been one of my greatest joys. It is a great privilege to be able to observe how they learn and find ways to support their learning. In the process, I have made mistakes, lost my patience, and learned a lot about my own learning style.

12. Be willing to change

All the characteristics I have listed up to now, point the way to this last one - a willingness to change, to being flexible and responsive. Living with children means living with constant change as they are always growing and changing. The ideas I had about homeschooling when Josh was 6 years old deepened and changed over the years. I had to let go of some assumptions and hold firm to others.

Sometimes, change can be devastating; sometimes, it can be exhilarating. Sometimes, it can be both. Whatever emotion we use to describe change, it is inevitable. It is a natural part of life; it defines life. One of the best things about being a homeschooling mother is that you are an active part of the changes your children experience as they grow. Being involved with so much change and growth, you can't help but grow and change as well.

CHAPTER 2
Creating A Homeschooling Learning Environment

The importance of play
Encouraging positive social interactions
A list of equipment, materials, and toys that facilitate play

Environment - *The New Lexicon Webster's Encyclopedic Dictionary of The English Language (Canadian Edition),* defines it as "surroundings, especially the material and spiritual influences which affect the growth, the development and existence of a living being." Create is defined as "to bring into being." When we homeschool, we need to bring into being material and spiritual influences that will support and encourage a child to gain mastery of the skills needed to function in the world. This is a pretty big order! It may look kind of scary, and yet we have been doing this as mothers since our children were born.

In this chapter, I want to share with you some of my ideas about how to create a learning environment conducive to homeschooling. Please keep in mind that each family will create their own unique environment; one that fits their needs. At the same time as each family will have a unique learning environment, there are some things that I think are important to include in all homeschooling learning environments. First and foremost for successful homeschooling is that children need to have a place to play and things to play with. Play is the "work" of childhood!

The Importance Of Play

We have a picture book, *How Tom Beat Captain Najork and His Hired Sportsmen* by Russell Hoban, that seems to me to capture the essence of homeschooling in quite a delightful way. Tom just "messes" around and doesn't seem to do any sort of studying. This bothers his aunt who decides to show Tom how foolish this is. She invites Captain Najork to compete against Tom hoping to demonstrate to Tom that he needs to spend time with more formal studies. Tom wins all the contests because he has "fooled around" with all sorts of things and is better able than the sportsmen to play the games.

Children need to play and fool around with things; it's an important part of learning. We in our North American culture have formalized learning to such a great extent (classes for babies and toddlers on how to do everything from singing to working a computer), that it may be difficult to accept that the time children spend "messing around" has any value whatsoever much less an educational value. Yet play, non-adult directed play, is vital to a child's intellectual growth and creative abilities. In order for us as human beings to understand things, we need to have a primary experience of what we are trying to understand. We need something to hang our experience on. "La experiencia es la madre de la ciencia. Experience is the mother of knowledge." Cervantes

The book, *Truckers* by Terry Pratchett about some nomes (this is how Pratchett spells this word) illustrates this point. Most of the nomes have lived inside a store building for many generations and cannot even conceive that anything outside the store exists; that there is an "outside." When a group of nomes come to the store who have lived "outside," it takes a long time for the store nomes to believe in the existence of this other kind of life which is another world to them. To then learn that all nomes came from a star and were travelling through space when they landed on the earth is beyond the comprehension of most of the store nomes. As they have only experienced life in the store, they cannot even conceive of "outside" much less other planets or stars.

Play gives children primary experience to draw on as they get older. A child learns about numbers and the one to one correspondence of numbers as he plays with Lego blocks, dolls, or other toys. A child who has not had experience manipulating objects and not been allowed time to observe the relationships of objects - i.e., that three objects are three objects no matter how they are arranged cannot understand the concepts of arithmetic. A child who has not experienced moving his body through space will have a hard time understanding gravity and velocity.

During play, children also integrate their experiences with the knowledge they have acquired and test out how the things they have heard or learned about actually work. Play provides children with opportunities to try things out. Building with Lego, blocks or tinker toys gives children a sense of how gravity works with small objects. Swinging, jumping rope, riding a bicycle, or riding on a merry-go-round are some ways to learn about gravity with their whole body. Learning with the body - somatic learning - is something that is basic to understanding. Children need many experiences with natural forces or objects so that they have a framework to later understand the intellectual concepts that describe the natural forces at work on our planet. Play - inside and out of doors, imaginary, mentally or physically active - is vital to a child's developing intellectual powers and creative abilities.

Clarisa Pinkola Estes, in her book *Women Who Run With The Wolves* discusses the importance of play in creative life. Play allows us to experience things for their own sakes, to see what will happen if this and that are put together or this and that are put here under this. Play leads to new discoveries not only for children but for adults as well.

Because my children have never gone to school, they have had lots of time to play. I found it fascinating to see the sorts of things they did as they played. When the oldest two boys, Josh and Noah were young (5 through 8 years old) among the many other things that they did, they loved playing with little cars. They spent hours racing them and kept track of which car was the fastest in which situation - statistics. Robin and Holly at that age played with families of little animals, Lego people, or stuffed animals - sociology. As Robin grew older, he, like his older brothers, played more statistically oriented games. It is only our formal educational system that divides the world into various subject categories. In life, as in play, there are no divisions. One thing leads to another, and children discover facets of the world that do not fall into neat and tidy categories as they play.

Children play in all sorts of ways and in all sorts of physical environments. I have seen little girls play in the shoe department of K-Mart, while their mom was shopping for shoes, creating an entire world within the space of a few minutes. Play is as natural and as necessary for children as breathing. Let's look at some of the things you can do to support and encourage your children in their play.

Creating Space to Play

Some families limit children's play to certain rooms in the house. Some families have no limit to where the play takes place as long as it doesn't endanger anyone. You need to find what feels comfortable for your family. I found that when my children were young, they liked to play close to where I was. As they grew older, they wanted more private personal space as well as common family space.

There are two main factors to consider when creating play space for children: safety - both physical and emotional - and materials.

Physical Safety:

Physical safety can be challenging when there are children of varying ages in a household. Small toddlers and babies do not understand why they cannot eat Lego pieces or that certain block structures are not meant for them to knock down. When I had both babies and older children, I established certain safety precautions for both the babies and the older children. It is important for a baby not to be endangered by small objects within his grasp. It is equally important for older children to know that their creations will not be destroyed.

We kept things like little Lego pieces in the older children's bedroom. The door was kept closed so that their creations were safe, and the babies were kept safe from swallowing things. This was OK for the younger children when they were babies. As they grew older, they wanted to be part of whatever was going on and began to express a desire to play with similar toys. This presented a challenge and required a lot of supervision on my part to ensure the younger child's safety, i.e., that he or she didn't swallow the small pieces.

Keeping play spaces safe for varying ages means that you need to do a lot of supervising. A 6 year old cannot always remember to pick up little objects that may be harmful for a crawling baby. It is important to state the expectations of the family - small objects need to be where babies can't reach them - and then help a child to follow this expectation. Setting up a separate play space for older children as I did can make it easier for this expectation to be carried out. Small objects can then be kept in private play space rather than in communal play space.

Safety issues can be a challenge. It means anticipating and thinking ahead. It also means supervising play. It is a great challenge to provide room for children's expression without compromising their physical safety.

Let me give you an example. My boys were always fascinated with sticks. When they were under 5, the rule was that sticks were never used in "pretend" fights. They just did not have the physical or emotional control to avoid hurting someone. As they grew older, we would have long drawn out discussions regarding the safety rules involved in "pretend" fighting using these sticks as swords. We finally agreed that they could fight with "real" stick swords against imaginary people. No matter how careful they would be, someone would get hurt if they were "pretend" fighting with each other. Neither one of them liked being hurt or hurting the other. Sometimes the one who was hurt would get so angry at being hurt that he would lose control and, instead of playing, begin to fight in earnest. Fighting pretend people was not very satisfactory, and we would start the discussion all over again and come up with new solutions such as using foam swords or other soft objects.

As you can see from this example, we tried to find a solution that would fit my need for the boys to play safely and their desire to play in a satisfying manner. We constantly revised and discussed how to do this.

There were some things that I was not willing to compromise on such as safety equipment: bike helmets when riding a bike; wrist, knee, and elbow guards and a helmet when roller blading; baseball helmets and athletic supporters when playing baseball; helmets when horseback riding; seatbelts when traveling in the car; etc.

The model you set for safety in your home shows your child that you are serious about safety. At the same time that you provide safety equipment/protection, you need to be aware that there are no guarantees that a child will not get hurt. We risk being hurt when we are actively engaged in living. Your job as a homeschooling mother is to provide as safe an environment as you can.

My children have had stitches; been knocked unconscious from falls; suffered sprained ankles and wrists; bruises; and cuts. These are part and parcel of playing, exploring, learning. In the process of learning, we have become more aware of certain safety hazards, and found ways to prevent further accidents of the same nature. There is no "perfect" environment where children can play risk free. Because as homeschooling mothers we have children in our care for many more hours than most mothers do, it is vital to provide as safe a physical environment as we can.

Emotional Safety:

As well as physical safety, we need to provide emotionally safe places for our children. We need to give clear guidelines to our children about how to appropriately express their feelings. Homeschooling, if you have more than one child, means that your children will be together each and every day. People have often asked me how I could cope - their own children fought so much of the time when they were home together. How did I manage with my children home **all** the time?

Because homeschooling siblings are with each other many hours of the day, the issues of how siblings relate to each other have to be addressed. There is no escape. The family value system needs to be defined. What is acceptable behavior needs to be clearly and constantly stated so that children can learn appropriate ways of expressing themselves. This is hard work. Limit setting - when you stick to the choices you have made about the tone, the atmosphere of your family environment - means hours of introspection, hours of discussion (both heated and calm between you and your children and your spouse or partner), and hours of self-doubt as you try to establish an atmosphere of respect and consideration.

In order to come to a clear picture of what defines a safe place - a place where children are protected from harm, both physical and emotional; a place where children are encouraged and supported in their endeavors - you will struggle to consciously define your value system. Sometimes parents who decide to homeschool in reaction to the strictness and lack of responsiveness of formalized public schooling throw out not only requirements for how to go about learning but also requirements about how to relate to others - the "anything goes" philosophy that says that children will sort out for themselves how to relate to others if just given a free rein. I have seen too much harm that comes from this approach. It looks to me like a way to chaos rather than a way to help children learn how to relate to each other. I know in my heart from years of being with children before being a mother and since I have been a mother, that in order for children to learn, they need to be safe.

To create a safe emotional place for children to play in our family we have these three rules.

1. No hitting, pinching, etc.

2. No name calling

3. Each person (and his or her belongings) needs to be treated with respect

Restraining children when they are angry and expressing their anger with violence toward others is difficult. It was difficult for me because I had to work hard to learn to use something other than violence (spanking) when I went over the edge in anger or frustration by my children's behavior. Our society is just becoming aware of the pervasiveness of violence. We find it reprehensible in many situations, yet we have not resolved our fascination with violence as a solution to a problem nor realized how deeply violent behavior is ingrained in our culture. Spanking a child is still considered by many to be an acceptable parenting tool.

I worked hard to learn how to set limits and stick to those limits instead of finding myself frustrated to the point of spanking because my children were not doing as I asked. I was motivated to do this hard work because it was clear to me that if I expected my children to not hit or hurt others when they were angry, I couldn't either.

Spanking a child is a signal for parents to find ways to increase their repertoire of parenting skills. Hitting is a simplistic way of solving a problem. It doesn't really solve the problem. It changes it and defines who is stronger and more powerful. The problem is still there. The problem may be a battle between a child's needs or wants and an adult's needs or wants. Spanking resolves the problem of who should get what by making it clear that the person with the most physical power is right. This is not a message I wanted to send to my children.

Becoming a more effective parent is such a big topic, that many books have been written about it and about how to break the cycle of violence administered to children in the name of discipline. I have listed the ones that I found particularly helpful in the bibliography. I won't go on at length here about spanking, but just mention a few things that helped me to change.

Please remember as you work to help yourself, your child, or children to find solutions to problems that do not include violence that you are doing something that is difficult, valuable and powerful. It is only by each individual making choices that do not include violence, that change will come. If you give your children tools and examples of how to solve problems without using violence, you are giving them a gift. You also give a gift to our whole planet. We desperately need a new way of looking at how we solve problems on our planet. There is no more "them" and "us." (There never has been.) We all breathe the same air, drink the same water and live on the same planet. We live in a large family - the earth's family. The work you do to help your family/your children to find ways to solve problems that treat each person with respect will have many positive repercussions.

By the time my third and fourth children came along, I had learned how to set limits without using spanking. I never spanked very often, but I wish I could say I had not done it at all. My earnest desire to change and my commitment to finding a new "language" of mothering skills made it possible for me to learn how to state my expectations. At the same time, I learned to accept, not just intellectually understand, that children are children and will need help to do those things they are asked to do.

I learned to really take the time it takes to count to ten before acting on any aggressive impulse. I learned to walk away if I couldn't cope. I learned that raising small children and being with them 24 hours a day was a stressful job and required all that I had - all the way down to the ends of my toes and beyond. I learned to look into my children's eyes and see the child and not the act that was driving me over the edge. I was fortunate. The cycle of violence I inherited was not an overwhelming one. I could stop. The material I quoted in the first chapter about forgiveness from *Mastering Your Hidden Self* by Serge King was very useful to me as I looked back and wished I had stopped spanking earlier.

Name-calling or verbal abuse is another form of violence that pervades our society. It may seem less destructive than physical violence but it's effects are just as damaging as physical violence. That's why I set the limit of no name-calling or verbal abuse. This did not mean that my children did not have angry feelings or yell at each other. It meant that when they were angry I helped them to find acceptable ways to express that anger - using words to describe their feelings, hitting a pillow instead of a brother, going outside and screaming, etc. We all learned together as they grew older and were more able to express themselves verbally rather than physically.

In the early years, I often felt that being a mother meant being a fireman putting out the fires of arguments and fury. Sometimes, I got caught up in the blaze and fanned the flames rather than putting out the fire. My learning curve of motherhood was often bigger than I would have liked.

Let me give you an example of limit-setting for both physical and verbal abuse. When I only had the three boys, some neighborhood boys came to play with Josh and Noah. The four boys played outside and had fun for a while. Then the neighbors started suggesting that they play some sort of game that involved teasing Robin. I was outside working in the garden and keeping an eye on Robin because he was only 18 months old at the time. He went from playing with a hose, being with me, to following his older brothers around. After the game was suggested, I could see that Josh and Noah were uncomfortable. They were 7 and 5 years old at the time. I intervened and said "The rules at our house are that if you play with someone, you do not pick on them or attack them. I can't let you play the kind of game you suggested." The neighbors decided to go home, and after a few more visits, by mutual decision, they no longer came to play.

Some people think that children need to sort this out for themselves and would find my intervention interference. I think that children need help to know what family values are as well as help to uphold those family values until such a time as they can be their own advocates. Their ability to do this happens as they grow older. I think it asks a lot of a 7 year old to be able to verbalize a family limit and uphold it without parental support.

People expressed their concern to me that by my providing such a protected atmosphere my children would not learn how to assert themselves as they grew older. The old "if you don't start feeding them with a spoon now, how will they ever learn how to use silverware" routine that many adults use to justify things such as introducing solids, making children learn something against their will, sleeping away from parents, stop nursing, etc.

I think the following story illustrates that this concern that was expressed to me was ill-founded. At the beach one summer, Robin (11), Holly (8), and their friend (11) were playing in the water. Near to where they were swimming, a man, who was drunk, was splashing water at a number of children. I was on the beach. I thought that as this man began to splash my children, that they were OK with this. Then I really noticed the looks on their faces and got up, ready to intervene. At the same time, Robin stood and faced the man and, with a great deal of forcefulness in his voice, told him to stop throwing the water. At the same time, Josh (17) had come closer on his air mattress and called the attention of the lifeguard to this man. Holly, crying, ran out of the water to me. The man responded with some nasty words. I said something to him and took Holly away from the water. The lifeguard came and told the man he needed to go sit on the beach for a while. Robin ran out of the water, and began to cry as well. Josh came up and we all talked about it.

I apologized to Holly and Robin that I did not notice sooner and do something. At the same time, I told Robin that I was proud of the way he had stood up for his sister, his friend and himself in such an assertive way in the face of such an uncomfortable situation. He realized that they did not need to accept this man's behavior, and acted on his realization.

It didn't surprise me that Josh did what he did, but it really surprised me that Robin told this man to stop. Even though he was only 11 years old, he could act to defend himself, his sister and his friend. He also knew that I was there to ensure his safety afterwards.

There were lots of adults on the beach watching this man and his buddy drinking beer, which is illegal in any public park in the municipality where we live, and throwing water at children. None of us acted to stop this man. Robin had the courage to face this man and tell him to leave him alone.

At the same time that we try to create a safe play space, one free of emotional and physical abuse or hazards, we must also be aware that life is not without risk. Life is not neat and tidy. We cannot make our children's lives risk free. As our children grow older, they will reach out to the world in all kinds of ways. We cannot prevent hurt, anguish, betrayal, and/or pain. We can be there beside our children when this occurs, validating their negative feelings as well as their positive ones and support them as they come to grips with less than ideal situations.

Our job as homeschooling mothers is to find a way to support our children in their reaching out while at the same time making it as safe as possible. We weigh the risks associated with an activity and try to decide if the benefits outweigh the costs. This is a skill that takes time and experience to master. It is a skill children must learn if they are to survive. How we model this skill helps our children learn.

Robin and Holly took horseback riding lessons. Horseback riding can be dangerous, so I looked for a teacher whose judgment I could trust. The teacher I found was someone I felt very comfortable with. I appreciated the way he worked with my children. He was aware of their limitations and never suggested that they try something unless he thought they could do it. He did not want to see them get hurt or the horses get hurt anymore than I did. If their teacher had pushed them beyond what I thought was reasonable, I would not have hesitated to speak up.

When my children have taken lessons in sports such as riding or gymnastics, I sat in on their lessons. It helped me to get a better sense of how a teacher worked with my children. I also made a point to ask my children how they felt about their lessons and their teachers. I wanted them to know that if they were uncomfortable with a teacher or situation or feeling unhappy but not able to pinpoint why that I would help them make a change.

It is important for a child to feel that a parent is still involved and on his side when learning outside of the family - that mom will make it safe. As my children grew older, they didn't need my actual physical presence whenever they participated in an activity outside of the family. However, they still enjoyed my willingness to watch them in their activities and needed me to be interested and aware of what they were doing.

As well as ensuring that a teacher is aware of physical safety, we need to be aware of the potential of other kinds of harm a child may suffer. I mention this because it is important to be aware that not all adults who work with children are "safe." We send out a lot of very mixed messages to children in our society. On the one hand, we warn them not to talk to strangers. On the other hand, many children have been raised by strangers since they were small by being placed in daycare centers. Or children go to classes and are expected to listen to and follow the instruction of these strangers. How can a child discriminate between a stranger who is OK and a stranger who is not?

Homeschooling gave me a great advantage in ensuring safety for my children, because they had me there to protect them. As they've grown older, they have reached out on their own no longer needing me to be present all the time, but still needing me as a sounding board to help them sort out what constitutes a safe, positive environment. Even older teens and those in their early twenties still need this kind of emotional support. Actually, we all need this kind of support whether from good friends, partners, or support groups. Make sure that your children know that you are still there to listen and support them in their judgments about people or situations. Children have been sexually and emotionally abused in sports, music, and other recreational programs. Stay in touch with your child and his or her teachers, coaches, instructors. Monitor how your child is feeling about his or her activities outside the home.

Creating a positive and safe emotional environment has been one of the most rewarding parts of homeschooling for me. It has not come easily. I labored to create a safe atmosphere for my children. I felt terribly isolated and alone at times. I often wondered if I was doing the right thing. Now that my children are as old as they are, I have no doubt that the work I did (and still do) to create a warm, loving, supportive, safe and creative atmosphere has paid off. The energy I used to "fill their tanks" with unconditional love by giving them my attention as described by Dr. Ross Campbell in his book *How To Really Love Your Child* has been returned many times over.

Finding Someone to Play With - Social Interaction

When we started to homeschool, I was often asked how my children would become "socialized" if they homeschooled. People don't ask me that any more. Perhaps in the years since Josh was a 6-year-old more and more people have become aware of the possibility of physical harm in school settings - such as school ground violence and drugs. This increase in the awareness of the possibility of harm has made it easier for people to accept that the socialization that goes on at school is not always positive.

Here are some suggestions of various ways you can provide opportunities for your homeschooled child to meet or play with other children.

First in terms of convenience and accessibility are siblings. Because we have four children, our children have had other children to play with. They enjoyed playing with each other when they were young and still enjoy playing with each other now that they are much older. Their games have changed. They don't play together as often, but they still enjoy it. They developed close and satisfying relationships with each other.

Second in terms of convenience and accessibility are neighborhood children. It may be that you live in a neighborhood where children play outside and your child can join in. Some homeschoolers have found this works well. Others have found that their homeschooled child is singled out for some teasing and razing because of the way he is educated.

Before arranging a social life for your homeschooled child, take time to think about just how much interaction with other children is necessary and/or valuable. Some children thrive on being with others, some fade with too much social interaction, and some are a mix of both. Take time to discover how much social interaction works well for your child. When my children were young and had, had a particularly good time with friends, they wanted to do it again the next day. Sometimes this worked, but often it didn't. Too much of a good thing, like a steady diet of chocolate cake, doesn't nourish even though it might taste good at first.

Children need time to be at home to have time to themselves. They need time to digest the experiences they have had. Mothers need time with children to be in touch with what they are thinking, experiencing, and learning.

At the present time in our society, we have come to believe that children do best in large groups of children of similar ages. I question if this is actually beneficial for children. As a species, we do not have babies in litters. Twins and triplets are the exception, singletons the rule when we give birth. I have an instinctive feeling that children do better in smaller groups than larger groups and that they need the presence of adults to help them learn how to relate to others.

Children do a lot of learning by observation and mimicry. A group with various ages such as a family, gives children an opportunity to observe how people of various ages relate to others as well as being able to help each other with learning tasks.

Learning how to relate to others is a skill that is developed over time, like any other skill such as reading. When your child is playing with another child, he learns how to be with other children, what makes him happy when he is with others, and what makes him unhappy. You can provide safety for your child by being there and letting him know that he is welcome to come and be with you if he is uncomfortable or unsure. You can help your child by sharing your observations with him. If you see that your son is hesitant to go and play with other children on a playground, you could say "I saw that you were standing and watching the children play at the park today." Your son may answer with a monosyllable or tell you how he was feeling. You can continue the conversation and give him words for what you think he might have felt if you think it is appropriate. "When I saw you looking at them, I wondered if you felt afraid/shy/hesitant to join them?" Giving your child an opportunity to reflect on his experience and feelings allows him to better know himself. Respect your child's pace in making social contacts and offer your help but don't push him into a situation he is not ready for. "Is there a way I can help you when we are at the playground?" Your support and encouragement helps your child learn about himself and his social experiences.

Some children like being in groups. Finding groups of children may prove a challenge if you are homeschooling. Observe your children and how they are responding to social interaction as you set up ways of meeting your children's social needs. Monitor their behavior and general state. Sometimes, when a child is playing with others in a group, he or she may be O.K. at the time, but once he or she is at home unhappiness, anger, sadness may be expressed. This is a time to talk and discuss what happened. Your child may not be able or willing to share his feelings right after something happens. Bedtime is often a good time to go over the events of the day. It's dark; there's a more relaxed atmosphere. Feelings are often shared more often at bedtime than at any other time of the day.

As well as siblings and neighborhood children, there are recreation center classes that can provide group interaction for a homeschooled child. Other avenues to explore are scouting, guiding, sports teams, church groups, or other group activities organized for children in your community. Sometimes group activities that worked for your child at one age may no longer be interesting to your child at a different age. Some homeschooled children have been welcomed into the nonacademic parts of a neighborhood school such as drama productions, band, orchestra, or sports teams. This may be something to explore especially if you live in a rural area. This can be a way for your child to make friends with children who attend school.

Continue to monitor how well your child is doing. Observe the behavior your child exhibits before, during, and after a group activity to help determine if you have stuck the right balance between group and family activities.

Remember as you help your child find playmates that it takes time to develop friendships. Like marriage, friendship is often easier if the people involved have similar interests and/or backgrounds. Many homeschooling children have found it easier to be friends with other homeschooling children. To go about finding other homeschooling families, check your local library for information about homeschooling support groups. If there is no such group in your community, you may wish to put up signs in public places announcing your interest in meeting with others interested in homeschooling.

What I am suggesting here is what I suggested in the first chapter - find or create a support network or system, and perhaps you will find children who enjoy playing with your children and vice versa. There is no guarantee that just because children are homeschooled that they will enjoy each other's company, but it can be a place to start. (Most of my children's friendships have developed from my involvement with La Leche League. Some of the children homeschool, some go to school.)

When meeting with another homeschooling family (or any other family) for the first time, it may be easier for everyone, if you meet in neutral territory, say a park. That way, if the children do not "click," there is less of an obligation. It can be easier for children to begin a friendship in a neutral territory especially when they are younger. In a park or at the beach, the equipment is public and doesn't belong to any of the children or families. Meeting in this neutral territory allows both families to assess if a friendship is possible.

Remember that even children attending school do not always

find friends. They have classmates and acquaintances, but many children attending school feel pleased if they have one close friend.

As a homeschooling mother, you are also a playmate for your child. The games that you play with your child are a valuable part of homeschooling. Your child needs your attention and willingness to participate in her life as much as she needs friends who are children.

When the oldest child in a family starts going to school, he may no longer be interested in being "friends" with his younger brothers or sisters. The chances for a friendship to develop between siblings can be undermined by the social interaction in school because of the focus on age peers. One of the benefits of homeschooling is that homeschooled siblings often provide each other with companionship and friendship that is rare for schooled siblings.

One of the things that I have noticed about homeschooled children is that they are able to cross age and gender boundaries when they play. They are able to play with children of varying ages, based on whether or not the children in question enjoy each other's company rather than whether they are the same age. My older boys played basketball, soccer, and baseball with Robin and his friend, Robert. Holly was included when she wanted to be. These four boys of varying ages had a good time together playing physically active games as well as more quiet games such as "Magic." For many homeschooling children, interest and compatibility determine their choice of friends rather than age or gender.

Adult life consists of relationships that are not limited to age peers and instead are more related to interest. Homeschooled children have a distinct advantage over schooled children in that they have the opportunity to experience relationships with people of all ages because they are not in school for six hours a day.

I referred earlier to my children playing together and being each other's friends. I do not mean to imply that homeschooling your children will automatically ensure that they enjoy playing with each other. You need to facilitate the possibility of their play by making sure they have time together and establishing guidelines to ensure that their play is "safe" as I mentioned at the beginning of this chapter. You may have children whose interests and temperaments are dissimilar. This makes creating a peaceful home a challenge. To create a home where the members of a family support and basically like each other is something worth working toward, even though it often requires more effort than you were expecting to give.

As I said earlier, it is important to take time to think about just what kind and how much social interaction with others outside the family you choose to have. It may be that seeing other children once a week is about all your 6 year old can cope with. That's perfectly normal. Some children do not enjoy being around other children very much. Other children thrive. You need to observe your child and your family and find what works best for all of you. You may not find a "best" friend for your child. It may prove difficult to find other children in your vicinity with whom your child "clicks." This also happens to children attending school and is not directly related to homeschooling. As long as your child has some people he talks with, relates to, plays games with, he will have an opportunity to learn about relationships. That's what socialization is all about.

Toys, Materials and Equipment

Before I begin this list of toys, materials, and equipment let me just say a few words about the value of having time to play outside in the natural world. My mom used to say to me frequently that "If you give children sand and water, they will always find something to do with it and be happy." I remember being taken to the beach when we lived in Holland. It was not an easy trip. It was a 45 minute walk. My mom pushed us in a buggy, carried us on her bike, or, as I got older, helped me to scoot along on a scooter while she pushed my younger brother and sister in a buggy. (I have a brother who is 2½ years younger than I am and a sister who is 4½ years younger.) I can still remember being in the dunes, then going and playing on the beach, jumping in the waves. When it was too cold for the beach, she took us to a wooded park that involved a similar walk. We lived in an apartment and had no yard.

After we moved to the U.S. when I was 8 years old, we still lived in an apartment with no yard, but there was a vacant lot next door where I would sometimes play, as well as a wooden porch over a set of garages. I had friends with yards where I played. My mom still took us to parks, walking there with us. She began working because my father could not find steady work. On the weekend, we still went to parks, lakes or an arboretum so that we could play outside in the natural world.

My father died when he was 44. My mom was 41 at the time and had three children 13, 11, and 9. She had to keep working to support us. Now that I am way past the age she was when he died, I have even more admiration for the decisions she made. She continued to take us to beaches, pools, the arboretum, and parks on week day evenings and on the weekends even though there were many household tasks that needed doing. She gave me two gifts: a connection with the earth and the natural world that I am thankful for everyday, and her presence as we played in the natural world. She made it clear that she valued us - our childhood and our need for time to play and have fun while she was with us, watching or participating.

So go out with your child into the rain, the wind, the storms, and the night as well as out on the sunny days. Even if you live in an apartment in a city, there are parks and bits of green that can give a child an experience with forces other than man-made ones. I think this is vital for children's well being.

With that said, let's move on to the toys, equipment, and materials that will help you create a stimulating learning environment. Let's start with books and a library card. Although I will write more about books in Chapter 3 and 6, I want to stress here the value of libraries. If you live in a rural area, bookmobiles may provide the services of a library. If that is not possible, there may be mail order library services available through a university near you. Whatever it takes, it is worth your while, no matter how small the library, to try to find access to one. What better deal can there be than a library card? The whole world of books available to you free or at nominal cost.

Now don't you wish there were libraries for toys as well? In some cities there are. In fact in some libraries, games and puzzles are available for check out along with books. In other places, parents have started toy libraries. Toy libraries usually require a subscription fee in order to join. Members often work cooperatively to manage the exchange of the toys. Toy libraries can provide things like Brio train sets without individual families spending hundreds of dollars to purchase a complete set. Toy libraries can also give you a chance to see what kind of toys have staying power for your child. Sometimes children are desperately anxious to have a toy and find out a week later that this toy is not really as thrilling or exciting as it seemed at first.

How does one go about finding the toys and other materials that will last for more than a week if there is no toy lending library available? I wish I had **the** answer. I don't. I do have some suggestions for basic toys that seem to work for most children some of the time. These are the ones that I will list. You will need to determine which toys suit your child or children, which ones fit your family budget, and which ones suit your family's value system.

When first reading this list, it may seem overwhelming and costly. Remember that no individual family starts out with all of these things, they are acquired over time. Birthday and other holiday gifts are often a time when children receive some of the more expensive toys or equipment that they enjoy playing with. Not all the things I list are expensive, nor do they need to be purchased new. We have found garage sales, thrift shops, and/or newspaper ads great places to find secondhand toys and equipment.

It is important for homeschooling children to have a variety of things to play with. They will spend many hours at home, playing with the things you provide. You need to provide a full, diverse, and rich environment for learning if you intend to homeschool because the early years of life profoundly influence creativity and intelligence. Scrimping on equipment, materials and toys is not a savings nor is it necessary to be independently wealthy to acquire these things. As I said above, thrift shops, garage sales, etc. are often filled with bargains such as board games, puzzles, dolls, trucks, etc.

Before going into the specifics of what toys I recommend, I'd like to suggest that you have family toys as well as toys that belong to individual children. Let me clarify. It is important for children to have their own things so that they have a choice about sharing. At the same time, it is important to have things that all the children in the family can play with. A set of wooden blocks is an example of a

family toy. One child may be playing with it and not want his cre-
ation destroyed, yet he understands that these blocks belong to the
whole family and will need to be shared with other children in the
family at some future time.

My husband and I ran a nursery school before our children were
born. The toys we had for this school as well as some of my husband's
childhood toys became our family toys. They were kept in common
areas of our house so that they were accessible to our children and
to visiting children. Having family toys meant that our children
weren't expected to share their own toys with visiting children unless they chose to do so. This may seem strange as one of the things
we want to help children learn to do is to share.

Imagine for a moment that someone who is a friend of a friend of
yours comes over to visit and starts using your kitchen cooking equipment or your sewing machine. It would feel like an invasion of your
privacy and boundaries. Asking children to share their toys or belongings with other children is similar. Children will learn generosity better by the ways in which their parents demonstrate generosity
than by being told to share their toys. When purchasing toys, ask
yourself, "Is this toy for a specific child that will become his own or
is this toy something for the whole family?"

Here's an alphabetized list of equipment, materials, and toys that
we have found to be an integral part of our learning environment.
This list is not meant to be complete. I included toys that we have
found to have "staying power." Please take time to observe what
your child enjoys doing. The addition of a new toy or piece of
equipment may open up a new direction for a child or support him
in an interest. It's fun to find something that your child really enjoys. It's one of the delights of being a parent.

I have listed mainly big sorts of toys. There are lots of little toys
- like magnifying glasses or marbles that can bring as much delight
and pleasure to a child as an expensive set of Playmobile. What
your child has to play with in part determines the kind of play that
he engages in. The more you can do to support your child's interest,
the more able your child is to pursue this interest. You let your child
know that his play is important when you provide him with suitable material and toys to play with. And, as I said earlier in this

chapter, play is very important for children. Toys are the tools of your homeschooling environment, necessary for your children to have so that they can develop their creative abilities.

Art and craft materials:

Colored Pencils - My children liked to use these. They each had their own set of 60 colored pencils as well as our family having a set or two. I like the kind that comes in box that will stand up so that you can see all the colors.

Craft materials - beads, fabric scraps (if you don't sew, you could post a note at a local fabric store asking for scraps), popsicle sticks, feathers, buttons, sequins, dried pasta, ribbons, old jewelry, etc. These are family items although my daughter, Holly, enjoyed receiving presents of scraps of ribbon, lace, buttons, etc. when she was younger.

Crayons - these do not get used very much at our house, but we have lots of them around. I can think of few things as satisfying as a new box of wax crayons! We used Neocolor II Aquarelle crayons by Caran D'Ache for face painting. These are water soluble crayons that wash off the face very easily. They are available in large and small boxes and often in individual colors. We use oil pastels and chalk pastels more frequently than wax crayons. They are bright and cover a lot of area very quickly.

Glue - Push up glue sticks are such a great invention! White liquid glue is good for some things, but we find that it is often just too slow. A glue gun with plastic glue sticks can be a very handy tool for older children. Beware because it's easy to burn fingers.

Modeling materials:

Bees' Wax - This is available in colored blocks specifically for modeling. It is very soothing to work with, leaving hands soft and smelling like honey! It does not get hard even when exposed to air. It only requires the warmth of your hands to make it pliable enough to work easily. Even very young children can use it with ease.

Clay - like playing with water and sand, clay satisfies an inborn need to mold and shape things. There is clay available that will air dry or clay that needs to be fired in a kiln. Often just playing with clay - wet, squishy, malleable - is all that a child wants. Making something that will be fired in a kiln isn't necessary every time you and your child work with clay. If there is a ceramics outlet nearby, you might ask them for suggestions about the kind of clay to use. Often these places will fire things for you as well. Clay requires more clean-up than mothers are often prepared to face. I kept a plastic tablecloth just for clay use as well as some sponges and wooden tools just for clay. It can be fun to go and dig clay if you can find a place in your neighborhood where this can be done and then shape things with the clay. Using clay can lead to all sorts of fascinating discussion about how people lived before there were stores.

Papier-Mâché - fun, messy, and recycles newspaper and other papers. We have used it for special occasions. Check your library for instruction books.

Plasticine - easily worked modeling material that stays pliable. We have used it as something to play with on long trips; each child had an individual package of thin strips of various colors of plasticine. We liked to look at Barbara Reid's illustrations, i.e., *The New Baby Calf.* She uses plasticine to "paint" with. This inspired us to try to use plasticine in this way.

Playdough - either the commercial kind or the kind made at home (see appendix 1 for a recipe) is lots of fun. It is an inexpensive modeling material and like clay satisfies an urge to shape and mold. I found it a useful ice breaker for children just getting to know each other - lots of playdough at the kitchen table and various tools such as plastic spoons or metal spoons, canning jar lids, butter knives and a garlic press to shape it, cut it, or mold it. It's also soothing for moms to play with; squeezing it through the hands releases a lot of tension.

Sculpey - a modeling material that can be baked in a home oven to a hard finish. We use a lot of this. It's easy to use because the material warms up very easily in your hand and becomes very pliable. My children have used it to make Christmas decorations, earrings, little toys, food for their Lego people, presents for their friends, etc. It doesn't stick to your hands, and bakes fairly quickly, 10 - 15 minutes at 250° F. We like it better than Fimo which is a similar material but takes a lot longer to become pliable.

Paint - Of all the kinds of paints we have, boxes of water color paints were used the most frequently. (August is often a good month to buy these things as stores offer "Back to School" specials.) I also liked to use large round blocks of water color. We sometimes did wax-resist pictures. I found it very handy to have a big block of black to use to cover the wax resist picture. When Josh and Noah were little, I had an easel set up and jars of tempera paints available at all times. (If you mix a bit of soap powder with the powdered tempera and water, it washes out of clothes more readily.) They enjoyed this very much. Acrylic paints are fun to use as well. They give a satisfying finish to wooden objects.

Paper - I think it is vital to have lots of good quality (as good as you can afford) blank paper available for your children. Although it would seem ecologically sensible to use the backs of other papers, such as office paper or computer paper, once your child begins to express himself in recognizable ways on paper, you never know when he will create something special. It would be so sad if it were on the back of a flyer or an old letter. For this reason, we have always had lots of 8½" x 11" blank photocopy paper and as well as larger sheets of paper available. It is now possible to buy paper made from recycled fibers. If you are still concerned about the waste because your children go through lots of paper, use the backs of your children's rejected art work for lists, letters, etc. This art work (no longer wanted by your children) also makes great wrapping paper for gifts.

As well as good paper in various sizes, our children liked to use sketch books. These are also available made from recycled paper. Check with art supply stores for inexpensive good quality paper. Let them know you are homeschooling, and ask if they will give you a discount. These stores are also good places to get origami paper and other specialty papers.

Another source of paper is printers. Look in your local yellow pages for a list of these businesses and ask them if they give away their offcuts. We have found printers to be a great source of all kinds of marvelous paper in odd sizes. Explain that you homeschool and need the offcuts for your schooling program. The printers that I have dealt with have been happy to put us on their waiting list for offcuts.

Balls We have lots of these in many sizes. Balls small enough to hold and throw easily; large balls with handles made especially to sit and bounce on; soft and squishy balls; hard balls; large, small, and medium size balls; and those tiny hard balls that bounce up ever so high. A can of new tennis balls was once a very welcome present for my boys not for tennis, but to play with. Nerf balls are great! My boys used the firm kind to play baseball with in our yard. We also have a nerf soccer ball that gets used for ball tag - the person who is *it* throws the ball at the others who are playing. If you are hit, then you are it. This ball doesn't hurt, unlike the rubber balls I remember playing dodge ball with as a child.

All of my children have liked balls: to carry around, to sit on, to play with, to throw, to own. We kept balls in boxes by the door. Until quite recently I kept a couple of tennis balls in the car, so that we could play catch if we were delayed unexpectedly.

Bicycle A bicycle gives a child wings. We've been lucky to find good secondhand bikes. It's important to remember that if a child is going to ride a bike, he must like the bike - like the way it looks, feels, and handles. It's important for a child to understand what the limits of the family budget are, so that he knows what kind of bike it is possible for him to have. Sometimes getting a bike of a certain kind is so important to a child, that he is willing to earn money to contribute to the purchase. Once you have a bike for a child, make sure that child also has a proper helmet and wears it!

Blocks   Although wooden blocks are usually thought of as a toy for younger children, older children can and do enjoy building with blocks as well. Blocks are a family toy in our house. We have had the floor covered in block structures for various reasons: to create a place for little cars; to create farms for plastic farm animals; or to create houses for dolls.

It is important to have a set of blocks that match, i.e., they are half or twice as big as others and to have more than one of each shape and size. We found it fun to make blocks out of end cuts of lumber to add to a basic block set. Wooden and plastic spools and wooden beads are also good additions to a basic block set.

Cars, Trucks, and Other Vehicles   Little "dinky" cars, tractors, big trucks, little trucks, new and used trucks are great toys for the imagination. Although Holly didn't "zoom" cars around when she was little like her brothers did, she sometimes played with them when she played with her dolls because one of her dolls liked to play with cars. Friction motor cars, cars that have sirens, trucks and tractors to be used in the sand are all fun. You can usually find inexpensive models as well as more expensive ones. Garage sales or thrift stores often have good selections at very reasonable prices.

Dolls, Puppets, and Stuffed Animals   Like balls, we have lots of these around the house. Our boys didn't play with dolls as much as Holly did, but they did play with stuffed animals, puppets, and little fuzzy plastic animals. All of these toys allow a child to be creative and engage in dramatic play. When Josh and Noah were about 9 and 7, they made a number of finger puppets with felt and needle and thread. They put on plays with these as well as with our hand puppets. Each of our children has also made a "Waldorf" type doll - a soft stuffed doll with a face that has just eyes and a straight line for a mouth.

The Pleasant Company dolls and Lissi dolls are soft vinyl dolls with cloth bodies. You can send for a catalogue from the Pleasant Company by going to their web site as well as writing or phoning them. Their dolls are expensive, but they are beautiful and have the sweetest faces. They make historical dolls as well as contemporary ones. The historical dolls have costumes and stories appropriate to their historical time. Pleasant Company, 8400 Fairway Place, P.O. Box 620190, Middleton, WI 53562-0190 USA. Phone number 1-800-845-0005 www.americangirl.com

Dress-up Clothes We keep a trunk full of dress-up clothes in our hall. What has been most useful are lengths of cloth - shiny, filmy, bright, dark, patterned and plain. These can be fashioned into turbans, capes, skirts, belts, loin cloths, etc. Imagination is the only limit. Garage sales, rummage sales, and/or thrift shops are good places to get things like fancy dresses, shoes, or wigs. Just before and right after Hallowe'en is a good time to acquire dress-up things such as masks, wigs, or face paint as stores put these items on sale then.

My children used our dress-up clothes to put on plays for us to watch or as they engaged in play themselves. They have pretended to be Roman centurions as well as people from medieval times or pirates. It amazed me how they created costumes for different time periods from the same materials.

It's important to have a place to keep all of these things, so that they can be found again. Although I prefer to store things on shelves rather than in large boxes or bins, our dress-up trunk works well. I was always amazed that everything fit back in and the lid closed after all the items had been taken out, sorted through, and used.

Games and Puzzles I will talk at length about games in Chapter 5, so please refer to that chapter for information about specific board and card games your family might enjoy. Games are an important part of a homeschooling curriculum. They provide children with opportunities to play within fixed boundaries.

Puzzles are a great way for a child to learn about patterns, matching shapes and colors, and spatial relationships. Start with simple puzzles. Once a child can do puzzles of 25 –60 pieces, try ones with more pieces. We found 250 piece puzzles to be the most satisfying. They can be completed fairly quickly but still present a challenge.

Lego   As the Lego company says "It's a new toy everyday!" We have family Lego as well as individually owned Lego sets. It is such a creative toy - children can play with it in all sorts of imaginative ways while they learn about structure and form. I recommend getting three or four basic sets as a family starter set because it's important to have enough Lego pieces so that you can build more than one structure at a time. Then as needed and wanted, you can add more specialty sets for individual children or the family.

My boys played with Lego almost everyday even into their teens. There is something so appealing in how easily the pieces fit together. When they were younger and played with Lego everyday, we talked about how much fun it would be to go to Denmark to Lego-land to see a whole town made of Lego. We enjoyed looking at the pictures in the book *The World Of Lego Toys* by Henry Wieneck. It was fascinating to read how Lego was invented and developed and how Lego is used by both adults and children all over the world. Engineers and architects use Lego when making prototypes for buildings. There are even some colleges/universities who ask an applicant to build a Lego structure as part of their entrance requirement. It's a great toy!

Plastic animals   Plastic animals add a lot to a child's creative play. As a child plays with these plastic animals, he can't help but absorb their details, the way they are formed. That's why it is important to have some animals that are anatomically correct and in proportion. It makes learning about animals just that little bit easier.

One of my favorite artists, Rien Poortvliet, in his book, *Noah's Ark*, describes the large wooden toy boat - a Noah's ark - that his father made for him to use with his Britain plastic toy animals. Poortvliet's book is a compilation of his drawings of all the animals on planet earth with a very brief story line. It's beautiful. He must have absorbed the shape of many animals during his play.

Playmobile   Holly and Robin enjoyed playing with Playmobile for many hours a day. They liked to play imaginative games and spent many hours having fun with this toy. Josh and Noah enjoyed building more, so Playmobile didn't suit them as well. We have used Playmobile people as part of Creche at Christmas time, dressing the people in costumes. It works well because they stand up so easily. Playmobile, like Lego, comes with lots of little pieces and can be quite challenging to keep track of. Some children like to keep their Playmobile in sets, ours gets stored all together in a large plastic bin - sorted by category (adults, children, hats, small animals, etc.) in various smaller plastic containers or plastic bags. I loved finding Playmobile or Lego at garage sales or thrift stores as it is so expensive when new.

One of the things that is most charming about Playmobile is all the details - such as the little mittens and skates, etc. that come with the skaters. It can also be a drawback as a child has to spend time sorting out where all the small pieces are in order to play. Certainly a good way to learn organizational skills!

Sand Toys   As I stated before making this list, playing with sand and water seems to bring joy to most children. Although you do not need more than your hands to play with sand and water, it is helpful to provide your child with a bucket and shovel. There are lots of other sand toys available. You can see what inspires your child. Give yourself a bucket and shovel, too. It's fun to dig in the sand and make sandcastles.

Sports equipment   I mentioned balls at the beginning - here I want to stress the need for providing equipment for big muscle activities. It is important for children to run about and move their bodies every day. Important for us as mothers, too. We have a small trampoline - a Rebounder - that has provided us with many years of service. Brisk walks, running around the yard or the block does not require anything special in the way of equipment. Sometimes it is more fun for children to exercise if they are playing a game - such as badminton, croquet, volleyball, soccer, tennis, or baseball. Skating with roller blades is also a great way to get exercise and have fun. Skipping ropes, small individual ones and long ones that are turned by others are another way to burn up lots of energy.

Tools   Learning how to use a hammer, screw driver, saw, wrench, etc. is necessary for functioning in the adult world. If you have these sorts of tools, it can be very satisfying for your child to work with wood and make things. Of course, until they become skilled at using these tools, you will need to provide supervision and instruction. Access to garden tools and a space to have a garden might also be appealing to some children. Learning how to use kitchen tools is also an important skill. Again, with supervision, children can learn to use blenders, mixers, ovens, etc. to create yummy things to eat. A sewing machine is another tool that a child can learn to use. Holly likes to sew doll clothes for her dolls. When she was 8-9 years old, she learned to use the sewing machine and created pants and shirts for her dolls. My boys also learned to use the sewing machine around that age and made things such as quivers for arrows.

I started this chapter with a reference to Tom and Captain Najork and messing around. Messing around is what my children have spent a lot of time doing. Their learning has been the organic kind - from their experience as well as from what I have requested that they learn. Through play, my children absorbed all kinds of information and drew all kinds of conclusions. In order to do this, they needed lots of time to play, including time to get bored. Homeschooling as we have done it has meant very little formal instruction and lots of play.

Through their play, Josh and Noah learned all kinds of things about how paper airplanes flew. They had bags and bags full of them when they were about 8 and 6 years old. We provided information with books about paper airplanes, answered questions when asked, and watched as they flew their airplanes around the yard. They observed how the wind, the humidity of the air, the shape of the wings, and the kind of paper they used affected the flight of their planes. This was all self-generated and maintained. It led them to keep mental statistics about which plane flew the farthest under what conditions. They had fun making different styles of planes with different paper. Through this playful activity, they repeatedly demonstrated their ability to focus, their ability to draw conclusions from their observations, and their ability to make relevant comparisons. Things that children in school are asked to do, but in the context of teacher directed activity rather than self-generated activity.

It is through play that a homeschooled child has the opportunity to explore what interests him, and to do it with fewer arbitrary interruptions. Coaches and teachers who have worked with my children, often commented on my children's ability to concentrate and focus on the activity at hand. Because my children have the freedom to play, opportunities to choose their play, and the freedom to learn through their play, they are able to make a commitment of time and effort when they set out to do or learn something.

Let me give you some examples: Robin started percussion lessons when he was 12 years old. In the first six months after starting the drums, his practice time grew longer and longer until he was practicing 2½ to 3 hours a day. He organized his day to ensure that he had this much time to practice. He made a commitment to practicing because he enjoyed it. It was playing - playing the drums. Because he practiced so much, he progressed rapidly and also rapidly increased the volume of the material he was playing.

When Robin played baseball, he also gave it his full attention. He played beyond the regular Little League season when he was chosen to play on a 10 year old tournament team. He found it surprising that some of the boys seemed to be unable to concentrate - instead they would throw their gloves up in the air or do other things that showed that they were not paying attention to the game when they were out in the field. Baseball is a slow game. It requires a level of attentiveness that stretches the attention span of many children.

Holly took some rhythmic gymnastics classes for a while. She enjoyed it for about four months and then decided that she didn't want to do it anymore. One of the things she commented on as she was trying to decide if she wanted to continue was that it seemed as if some of the girls didn't really want to be there. They would not follow instructions or do just the bare minimum of what was asked. Holly wondered why they kept coming. A good question!

When Josh and Noah were 6 and 4 they took gymnastic lessons. They listened and followed instructions. They wanted to learn how to do gymnastics. They loved the classes and the instructor became a very special person in our lives. She commented frequently on Josh's and Noah's attentiveness. She found it easy to teach them because they paid attention. They never expected to do anything but pay attention as they wanted to be there to learn gymnastics.

My children's ability to be attentive comes from having the freedom to choose their activities, and follow their interests. My children know that when they choose to play a musical instrument (or participate in some activity) they are doing it because they want to do it. I will support them and help them. They know that I delight in the music that fills the house. However, from the beginning, they determined when they practiced and how long they practiced. Their practice is their play. It brings them great pleasure. It is a continuation of what they did when they were younger, just a different form of play.

As you have read this chapter, I am sure you have concluded that I think play is very important! Give your child lots of opportunities to play. Ensure that there is playtime each day. People have often asked me just how I can manage to teach four children. I explain that most of the time my children play. Like a good nursery school teacher, I facilitate play by ensuring that our house is a safe place to play, there are things and/or others to play with, and then I stand back and let my children play. In between play times, I read stories, have discussions, or help someone learn to read, write, sew, cook, or do math, etc. but by and large my children play.

This may be hard to visualize - after all most of us went to school for 12 years and spent hours learning and memorizing facts, information, and ideas. How could children possibly be ready to face the adult world if all they do is play? I don't know how to explain it, I just know that it has worked in my family, and in other homeschooling families that I have known. Recognizing the importance of play, encouraging children to play by creating an environment in which play can take place means trusting that children are inherently good and want to become competent in the world. It means trusting the natural progression of their abilities and their desire for more understanding and knowledge.

I think about Gerald Durrell, the founder of the Jersey Preservation Trust. He wrote a number of books about his childhood years on the island of Corfu where he lived with his family in the 1930s. He was 10 when they moved there, 16 when they left. He explored the flora and fauna of the island to his heart's content. Although he had tutors at various times throughout those years, he was allowed the freedom to pursue his interest in natural history. He observed the lives of the animals and people around him, and had many opportunities to engage in conversations with people of all ages. From the stories he tells in his books, he had very few contacts with children his own age. Instead he had time, lots of it, to play. He once said that he wished he could give every child the gift of the childhood that he had, had on Corfu. He was fortunate, he discovered his passion, his calling in life, while he was young and he was allowed and supported as a child to pursue his interest.

Your child may not discover his passion or vocation early in life, but by giving him time to play you can support him to discover and then follow his interests. Who knows where that will lead?

Holly 1990

CHAPTER 3
Helping Your Child Learn to Read

Ways to help your child learn to read
Beginning reading books

Teaching a child to read is one of the major tasks of education. There are many methods to teach reading and there are many theories about how children learn to read. I will focus on how you can help your child learn to read at home in this chapter: how to motivate children to want to read, the signs of reading readiness, and suggestions of how to work with your child to enable him/her to learn to read. I hope that reading about my experiences with my children as they learned to read will help you. Please keep in mind that each child is unique - what works for one child may not work for another.

Before a child can learn to read, he needs to want to read. His experience with books and stories help determine his attitude toward learning to read. If his experience is positive, i.e., stories were read aloud to him at bed time or other times of the day and he saw the adults around him read, learning to read will be easier. It will be easier not because the act of learning to read will be easier, although it might be, but because the child has experienced that reading brings pleasure. It has built in rewards. This positive experience with the printed page helps to balance the work of learning to read and makes the effort worthwhile.

Reading is and has been one of my greatest pleasures. As a child I loved going to the library and coming home with new stories to read. I hoped that my children would come to enjoy reading. To that end - to help our children associate books with pleasure - my husband and I read aloud to them starting when they were very young (under a year old) and continuing into their teen years.

The books I read years ago about reading and how children learn to read seemed to say that given time, a child would just naturally begin to read if read to. Working under that hypothesis, I did a lot of reading aloud. When everyone was little, I read stories aloud at least 2-3 hours a day as well as telling or reading a story at bed time. Story time was a great way to soothe unhappy children. It gave us all quiet time together and a chance to recover our equilibrium. It was also a good way for me to spend time with older children as a younger one was sleeping or nursing.

These story times changed to bed time reading. I read to my children every night until they were well into their teens. Even though they could easily read what I read aloud and had often heard it once, sometimes twice before, they still listened. It was time together we all enjoyed.

Just as it is important for children to have positive experiences with books before learning to read on their own, reading aloud needs to continue beyond the time when a child can read on his own. Jim Trelease, author of *The Read Aloud Handbook*, writes about the importance of reading aloud to children of all ages. If you haven't already seen his book, you may find it helpful as he suggests many read aloud titles. I have listed some of our family's favorite read aloud books both within the text of this chapter, Chapter 6, in the Bibliography, and in the Appendix.

One of the reasons to continue to read aloud once a child has learned to read for himself is that the time spent together while you read aloud is a special time. It's important to make it clear to a child who is learning to read that he will not lose that special time with you when he masters reading, instead he will gain access to the world of books on his own. Reading aloud to children helps them to hear how language is phrased. It gives them a chance to hear words they may not be able to pronounce, and it allows them to listen to stories they may not yet be able to read on their own.

In order to learn to read and be literate, a child must be able to feel comfortable with language - to be able to predict what might come next, as well as learn how letters make sounds that make words. This is why reading aloud can be so helpful for children. They hear how words are used to tell a story. English is not an easy language to learn to read. There are so many exceptions to the rules of pronunciation. It is also a challenge to learn to read because the symbols that represent the sounds of language (letters) seem to have no rhyme or reason to the way they are shaped.

I found that as my children grew older, they did not, as some children I had read about, teach themselves to read by age 6. When Josh was 7½ years old, I began to feel uncomfortable that he was not reading on his own. I started to help him learn to read. We worked on phonics about 10 minutes a day. He was my first child, so I learned as much from the experience as he did.

At the start, I asked him to read one word on a page. He enjoyed the early reading books that rhymed such as the Berenstain Bear books about Papa Bear's errors and the book *More Spaghetti, I Say!* by Rita Gelman. He could easily predict what the word would be at the end of a phrase in these rhyming books and enjoyed reading that word aloud.

We moved on to more words as Josh was willing, ready, and able. Throughout this whole learning process, I wanted the way in which he was learning to read to be pleasurable. I did not want learning to read to be boring, a chore, or a matter for anger or argument between us. I kept looking to Josh's responses and reminding myself of my goal - that he learn to read with pleasure. I would remind myself that learning needs to take place in a pleasant atmosphere. I would remind myself that it was not a life threatening situation that he was not reading at 7 ½ -8 years old. Reminding myself of this and keeping my patience took a great deal of effort and discipline on my part. Just as I was asking my child to learn a new skill - reading, I was learning a new skill - helping my child learn to read.

When Josh was 8½ years old, he started reading *Charlotte's Web* by E.B. White. He jumped from easy-to-read books to books with many chapters because all of a sudden, it all clicked and he understood. He could read! He wasn't just carefully putting the letters together to form one word at a time, he saw whole words and could read sentences. This "clicking" with reading is what seems to happen when children master reading. For some children, it never comes. Although they can piece together words, they are not literate, they do not find pleasure in the printed word; the words do not flow off the page and into their minds.

I would love to know just how a child all of a sudden understands how reading works. I think of it as an "Aha experience" (an expression used by Martin Gardner author of various mathematical articles and books including a book called *aha! Insight* about sudden leaps in understanding). I would love to be able to see just how this shift takes place. I have asked my sons, but they can't remember. Robin tells me that "Just all of a sudden I saw how it all worked and I could read just about anything. Now there is no way I can see a group of letters and not read what it says, as long as it is in English."

I hoped that Noah, Robin, and Holly would learn to read on their own, but when they turned 7½ - 8 years old and hadn't started to read, I helped them start the process of learning to read. Robin, like Josh, began reading fluently by the time he was 8½-9 years old, reading way beyond his grade level. Noah read fluently by the time he was 12½ years old. Holly made the transition from struggling to sound out the words to reading fluently when she was almost 11 years old.

It was worrying and uncomfortable for me when Noah was struggling to read. He so obviously found it frustrating and nerve wracking that I stopped asking him to read aloud to me after we tried it for a period of three to four months when he was 8 years old. He would read aloud a page or two of very simple beginning reading books, but he was so often unsure and hesitant. I reminded myself time and again of my philosophy of homeschooling - that children will learn when they are ready. I had to learn restraint and patience, and accept that Noah would learn at his own pace. He listened to many stories. His vocabulary was above what was expected for his age. His comprehension, his thought processes, and verbal communication skills showed that while he wasn't ready to learn to read, he was not a "slow learner." He just wasn't ready to read.

At 8½ years old, Noah began to change the size of the figures in his drawing after a few art lessons from a friend of mine. Noah had always drawn small detailed pictures. At 8½, he began to draw bigger pictures. He began to paint portraits from photos of Rembrandt's work as well as portraits from life at age 9½ - 10. His gift for art was evident in all he drew or painted from that age on. At 8, 9, 10, and 11 years old, he was not ready to limit himself to seeing things only from left to right and from top to bottom as one must when one reads. He needed time to let his artistic talent develop - time to be free of the pressure to limit his vision the way reading can limit it. I have heard and read that elementary school teachers have noticed that children's art work often takes a turn for the worse after they start to read. It becomes more stilted and limited.

There are many children who struggle to learn to read at age 8, 9, 10, 11, and 12 years old. Not all of them are artistically gifted. It may be that for those children who struggle with learning to read that there are reasons for their difficulty with the printed page that we haven't yet discovered.

I don't think we know enough about how learning to read changes a child's perception of the world. I don't think we know enough about what learning to read does to a child's capacity for oral memory. People who live in a culture with an oral tradition have a capacity for memory and observation that seems almost super natural to those of us in the literate world. I think we need to give children who struggle with the printed word time to develop at their own pace. Rudolph Steiner, a German philosopher who wrote about education as well as many other things, labeled learning to read as becoming linear. In the Waldorf schools which are based on his educational philosophy, children are not expected to learn to read (to become linear) before they are 9 years old or older.

I once read about some white men in the Arctic having trouble with a snowmobile. Even though the men who were riding the snowmobile had the diagram that explained the wiring and workings of the engine system, they could not figure out what was wrong.

An Inuit man asked them what the problem was. He took hold of the plan upside down, looked at the engine compartment and instantly discovered what was wrong, fixed it, and the snowmobile was working again. In the Arctic there are no fixed places for locating things, one needs to have an almost aerial perspective to be able to locate oneself in space. The Inuit man saw immediately where the diagram and the actual engine didn't match. He saw the engine compartment in a different way than the men who were having trouble with the snowmobile. This story gave me comfort when Noah didn't seem to be making any progress in learning to read. I drew comfort from this story because Noah was so adept at reading diagrams such as Lego instructions as well as so adept at art. He was obviously capable - he just wasn't ready to limit himself to being linear.

We may be doing children a disservice when we ask them to read when they are not developmentally ready to do so. We may be making it very difficult for children to develop their own individual ways of perceiving the world. Yes, I know that being literate is necessary in our culture, and that being able to read is vital for adult survival in our world. At the same time, I don't think we need to be in such a rush to push a child who is obviously struggling. I think that if we give a child time, a child who is raised in a literate environment will more than likely learn to read. We need to trust that our children have an inherent desire to become competent in the world. If a child is struggling to master the skills of reading or refuses to even try, it often backfires when we push.

Children struggle with learning to read for a reason. Patience is vital when you are helping your child learn to read as is a belief in a child's inherent desire to become competent. Many children are forced to learn to read before they are ready and they associate reading with drudgery, struggle, and humiliation. These children grow up to become adults who don't read. There are many adults who can read but do not choose to read even one book a year.

One of the reasons I chose to homeschool was to ensure that my children's self-esteem was not destroyed by agendas set for my children by others. So often children who are struggling with learning to read struggle because they are being asked to work within someone else's time frame. The reasons a child is not ready to read can be varied. It may be that a child has a need to develop his artistic vision, as Noah did. It may be that a child needs to develop other sorts of skills before turning to the task of reading.

The printed word doesn't have the cues of the spoken word - voice tones, body language and breathing patterns. Some children may rely on the nuances that these clues provide more than others, making it hard to understand the printed word.

Some children do not think in words, they may think in flashes of insight, in feelings, in visual perceptions, in colors, in music, etc. Before a child is ready to start reading, he needs to be able to think in words. A child may be experiencing the world in a certain way and then translating that experience into words. To add learning to read to the process of learning how to think in words may be an overload to the system.

I think this is what went on for Noah. He was able to communicate quite well, but I don't think his primary internal language - his thinking process - was in words, it was in pictures or some sort of visual language.

Children may also need to sort out how they hear words. They may hear words much differently than how the people speaking to them think they are pronouncing words. Let me give you two examples of this. When Josh was working with beginning reading books we came across the word "just." He was quite surprised at the way it was spelled as he had always assumed the word was "dust." He was sure that whenever I used the word, I said it as "dust" as in "Dust a minute." We had a long drawn out discussion about this. It upset Josh to have to change his perception of this word. I am thankful that I could be gracious and supportive while he struggled to accept that what he had interpreted all these years as "dust" was actually pronounced as "just."

A friend of mine was asked to read something that her son, who was 10 years old at the time, had written - "Chrick or Chreet." It was Hallowe'en, so she figured he must be writing "Trick or Treat." "Yes," he replied, "that's what I've written." He told her that that's how he heard it and he pronounced it for her as he had written it and said that that's how she pronounced it, too. It would be easy to get into

an argument with a child and tell him that "Of course I don't pronounce the words that way. You are just hearing it that way and you
are wrong," but it wouldn't serve any purpose. Denying the validity
of a child's perception is pervasive in our culture, it damages many
children.

If you discover that your child has interpreted a sound differently
than you thought you pronounced it - be gracious and empathize
with that child. It is confusing enough for a child to learn that his
interpretation is not correct. He needs support not negative comments about his abilities.

You can help your child master the skills of reading by building
on his or her inherent talents and strengths, and take into account
any weaknesses. This is when you draw on the observations you
have made of how your child learns. As a homeschooling mom, you
can work one on one with your child. You can tailor how you help
your child learn to read to suit the child. That's why I stopped
asking Noah to read aloud to me. He just wasn't ready to read on
his own. Both my husband and I continued to read aloud to him.

When Noah was ready to read at age 12, he began to read with
ease, not aloud, but to himself. At that time he was able to incorporate a linear focus without strain. I hope that reading about Noah's
experience with learning to read will help you as you help your
child learn to read. I hope it will encourage you to work with your
child at a pace that feels comfortable to both of you and help you to
accept that reading readiness does not happen at the same time for
every child.

Reading readiness has many components. Some of the characteristics (not necessarily acquired in the order presented) that each
of my children showed before they began to read voraciously on
their own were:

• they could think sequentially

• they knew how to recognize and form the letters of the alphabet

• they had a fairly stable understanding of the sounds associated
with each letter of the alphabet

• they thought in words

• they began to notice the printed words all around them.

My children acquired some of these characteristics at an early age - years before they started to read. My children knew how to write their names and the names of everyone else in our family by the time they were 3 or 4 years old. They knew how to form the letters of the alphabet but didn't necessarily know the names of the letters. I named the letters by the sounds they made rather than calling a letter by it's name. A woodblock alphabet, *Farmer's Alphabet* by Mary Azarian, was the source of the words I used to illustrate the sounds. (She designed this for her grade 1 classroom in rural Vermont.) "T (using the sound the letter made rather than the name of the letter) as in toad, etc."

When I started helping Josh, Noah and Robin learn to read, we used the beginning reading books that rhymed. I would point out how the word looked as they read the word at the end of a phrase. They could tell what the word would be because it rhymed and was easy to guess within the context of the story. We then moved on to working with homemade books of goofy stories based on simple phonetic words. "The cat sat on the fat rat on the mat." After a few months, Josh and Robin knew which sounds the various letters of the alphabet made. For Noah, it was too confusing. From his point of view the letters p, d, or b were the same letter viewed from different orientations. Holly had this ability as well. They were not able to limit their perception at age 8½ to seeing these letters as being separate. This coupled with the confusing phonetic rules of the English language was too much for both Noah and Holly at that age. However, Josh and Robin were willing to put up with the lack of logic and worked through our many beginning reading books when they were 8-8½ years old.

When I think back, I can still hear Josh read aloud a story about a little goblin from *Little Bear's Visit* by Elsie Minarik and Rita Gelman's *More Spaghetti, I Say!* Both of these stories have a sense of humor that appealed to Josh. I can hear Josh's dramatic expression and see his big brown eyes as he read these stories with ease, delighting all of us with his new found skill. As I mentioned before within six months Josh was able to read *Charlotte's Web* to himself, one of his favorite stories at that time. He then read whatever he found interesting. If it was beyond his comprehension, he didn't finish it. If it was not to his liking, he didn't finish it. I never checked to see that he understood what he read nor did I censor what he read. He read so much when he turned 9 that Noah was quite often disgusted because Josh wouldn't play with him.

Robin especially enjoyed the early reader *Hand, Hand, Fingers, Thumb* by Al Perkins. The repeating rhymes and rhythm "Hand Hand Fingers Thumb - One thumb One thumb Drumming on a drum - One hand Two hands Drumming on a drum. Dum ditty Dum ditty Dum dum dum." made it easy to memorize. Robin (and later Holly, too) read the book aloud to me many times. (I had forgotten how much Robin loved this book until I started writing this chapter. I began to laugh because Robin was practicing on his drumset as I wrote.)

Both my husband and I read many of the easy to read books to our children when they were quite young. That meant that when they were ready to start reading on their own, they could chose a familiar story. We have especially enjoyed all the Little Bear books by Else H. Minarik; the books about Oliver and Amanda Pig by Jean van Leeuwen; the books about Frog and Toad by Arnold Lobel; the books about the Berenstain Bears that rhyme by Jan and Stan Berenstain; and the Nate the Great books by Marjorie Weinman Sharmat.

Your librarian can help you find easy to read books. Then you and your child can find books that you enjoy. As well as using the library, it is important to have books of your own. We have found many beginning reading books for sale at garage sales and in thrift shops.

Part of learning to read is being able to anticipate what the author might say next, being able to think like the author. I became aware of this component of reading readiness while learning to work the word processor I used to write the first edition of this book. I had to think in the ways that it was programmed. In other words, whereas I might have made the machine's cursor move in ways that seemed much more logical and direct to me, I couldn't change the program. I learned to fit my thinking into the boundaries of the program.

When a child is learning to read, not only is that child learning to recognize the shape of the letters and the sounds those letters make, the new reader also has to think like the author of the book. Finding material that fit each of my children's thought patterns or ways of using language was a challenge.

Holly enjoyed working on her reading using the Little Bear books. The stories suited her way of operating in the world, the way she views things. Josh much preferred the Berenstain Bear rhyming books. The humor and rhythm of the verse appealed to him and suited his way of communicating.

That's why we have many kinds of early reading material in our house. Some author's thought patterns "fit" more easily with some children's thought patterns. To have to think in a way foreign to natural thought patterns as well as struggle to remember which letter makes which sound can make learning to read harder than it needs to be.

When I first began helping Josh learn to read I wasn't aware of this. I tried to find material that he enjoyed reading. As my other children learned to read, I began to observe how differently each of them think. These differences give diversity to our family life, enriching us.

Bio-diversity is now recognized to be important for our survival on this planet. We recognize that we lose something precious when some of the myriad forms of life that inhabit the Earth become extinct. I wonder if we need to think about the diversity of human perception, intelligence, creativity, and thinking as well. Are we eliminating human diversity when we force children to read before they have established their own unique ways of thinking and perceiving?

Holly and I started working formally on her reading one morning while we were at Josh's harp lesson. I had brought with me photocopied pages of an illustrated alphabet from *Why Johnny Can't Read* by Rudolph Fleschman. I asked Holly to look at the pictures next to the letters. (I covered up the picture of the gun for the letter "G" with a goat.) I explained how the picture related to the letter sound, e.g., egg for the short "e" sound. I then asked her to draw me a secret one word message using the pictures to sound out the word. I thought the idea of a secret message might appeal to her. She had wanted to learn to read about a year before and was overwhelmed by all that was involved in recognizing the sounds the various letters made. She was hesitant to try anything else for a long time. She liked writing one word notes to herself or her dolls with invented spelling. I hoped writing a secret message to me using pictures would give her a way to move beyond her hesitation. It did. I closed my ears and eyes while she consulted with Robin.

After decoding her message, I made up a message for her using the pictures for the sounds of the letters. We continued making up secret messages for the rest of Josh's lesson time, laughing and having a good time. We continued this message writing over the next few days until Holly could consistently match the sound to a letter. We then went on to use the lists of simple three letter words provided in the back of *Why Johnny Can't Read*. Holly enjoyed the challenge of reading these words. The ones she mastered, I wrote on individual 3" x 5" cards and put in her "Word Box" (a file box, a suggestion from *Games For Reading* by Peggy Kaye. This book has many suggestions for fresh approaches to reading games written by a teacher who works with children who have been labeled as slow learners or unable to read.)

From this beginning, Holly began to read basic early readers. One of her favorites was *Sounds I Remember* edited by Bill Martin. (The teacher's edition of any of the Sound's readers published by Holt, Rinehart and Winston, Inc. New York, N.Y. has useful information about how important memory is for learning to read as well as a discussion about how important it is to have early reader stories grouped into "chunks of meaning" to make it easier for a child to learn how to phrase what is being read. It is worth looking for a teacher's edition of one of these readers. Try your local public elementary school and ask if they can help you.) She also loved *A Kiss For Little Bear* by Else H. Minarik. She read aloud to me about 10 minutes every day, sometimes longer depending on her interest. I helped her pronounce words when she got stuck. She was willing to have me correct her. Josh and Noah did not like to be corrected or helped, which meant that I had to learn to be very quiet and only offer suggestions when asked. It was very hard for me to learn to do this.

Holly read to me for 10 minutes a day for about four to five months, then stopped wanting to read aloud to me. About 6-8 months later when she was about 9½ years old, she began to read on her own. She rushed into the room where I was to tell me that she had read 1½ pages in her book *"B" Is For Betsy* by Carolyn Haywood all by herself. She was very excited and pleased with herself. She then began to notice and read the signs when we went to the store or when we drove down the street. She began to think that she could make sense out of the words that she saw and so she noticed them. She began to spontaneously read words aloud. At age 10½, she read *Little House In The Big Woods* by Laura Ingalls Wilder to herself. She, like Noah, needed more time to switch to a linear way of thinking.

One of the things that was important for each of my children as we worked together on reading was that they retain ownership of the process of learning to read. I needed to observe and respond to their signals that told me that they had, had enough. This required awareness on my part. I found it a constant challenge to know when to suggest that we continue and when to let go and stop because a child could not do anymore. I looked for signs of exhaustion, boredom, anger, or frustration and worked hard to ensure we stopped before these set in. I sometimes asked them to read just a little bit more when it seemed to me that things were going well and they were enjoying it. If they were willing, we would go on, sometimes for a very long time. If they were not willing, then we stopped. I would ask this after our 10 minute working period defined by setting a kitchen timer.

I did not use this 10 minute working period everyday. We would do it daily for a week, then skip a few days and then start again. Then we would stop again for as much as a week or two and then start again. When both Holly and Noah clearly did not want to do even 10 minutes of reading each day, we stopped.

As a homeschooling mom, I could accommodate my children's individual needs and tastes as they learned to read. As we worked together, I had the opportunity to observe my children closely, to learn about how they learned, and to listen to what interested them.

We continued to build our relationship. When I asked them to do reading work that tore down our relationship, I realized that I was on the wrong track. Learning to read, unlike doing chores, was not necessary for the well-being of our family. Learning to read was for their individual benefit. They had a choice about learning to read. My children are now all avid readers. "I just love reading," Holly told me spontaneously on her way to a choir practice when she had just turned 11.

Josh reading to Robin

CHAPTER 4
Writing

How to encourage children to write
When to start, expectations, the mechanics of writing

Along with learning to read comes learning to write. When I was in elementary school, learning to write meant having standard cursive handwriting as well as being able to print neatly and legibly. I remember the hours that were spent on penmanship, spelling, and grammar. At the time I thought that the writing I did in school provided an opportunity for my teachers to tell me what I was doing wrong - how poor a writer I was. It never occurred to me that it could have been an opportunity for a teacher to acknowledge that I had something to say and to help me find a better way to say it. I never seemed to get the feeling that I was being asked to write because it was a way to communicate, to express myself. Instead, I felt that I was being asked to demonstrate that I knew the rules of grammar, could spell correctly and had a good vocabulary. I was sometimes found lacking in those skills. I have struggled to overcome the image I formed of myself during those elementary school years that

I could not write well and that therefore I had nothing worthwhile to say.

Since the mid 1980s, the focus in some elementary schools has shifted to help children express themselves in writing rather than to focus so extensively on the rules of written language at least in the early grades.   Invented spelling and whole language learning became a part of many elementary school curricula. In the late 90's and early 2000, there is another swing and a new emphasis on grammar, spelling, and more of a focus on phonics. With each swing of the pendulum, a little is left behind. I think one of the pluses of homeschooling is that you are much more aware of your child's learning style and can tailor the approach to suit your child. There's now a lot more material available to help you find what works best for your child. And, as Martha Stewart says, "It's a good thing!"

You, like me, may also have experienced a lot of criticism for the mechanics of your writing when you were a child in elementary school and find yourself worrying about spelling, punctuation, and grammar more than you expected to.

I try to keep this in mind:

T.T.T.
Put up in a place
where it's easy to see
the cryptic admonishment
T.T.T.

When you feel how depressingly
slowly you climb,
it's well to remember that
Things Take Time.

A poem by Piet Hein from his book *Grooks*.

It is important to realize that competency in the techniques of writing come with practice and interest. Like learning to talk, learning to write takes time. It is important to support all of your child's efforts at written expression. If you constantly correct your child's writing and focus on what's wrong rather than read for the content, your child may feel discouraged and be hesitant to try again.

As I helped my children learn to write, I tried to remember that the mechanics of writing were just that, the mechanics. These mechanics would improve over time. With practice my children would become more skillful at penmanship, spelling, and grammar. I tried to keep in mind that in verbal communication spelling is not a problem. My children knew which "there, their or they're" they were using in conversation even if in writing they got mixed up.

A spell check function of a word processing computer program can be a wonderful teaching tool. I like to know as I'm typing that I've misspelled a word so that I can ask for an immediate spelling correction. This works well for me because it is immediate. I've learned to spell a number of words this way that I used to misspell before. I like the immediacy and impersonal quality of the spell check function. I don't feel that the machine is belittling me because I don't know how to spell a word. It is only alerting me to the fact that this word is not stored in its system. I like to keep this in mind when I help my children with their writing. There is no need to assign blame or shame because a word is misspelled. Of course, computer spell checks do not correct words that are spelled correctly but are not in context such as homonyms. One needs a human proofreader for that.

My purpose when helping my children learn to write was two fold - to help them express themselves and to enable them to express themselves in writing by helping them learn the mechanics of writing. Balancing the two was a struggle. I think that the major function of writing is communication, so my first priority has been to encourage my children's expression.

My boys showed very little interest in writing things down. When Josh was first starting to learn to read and write, I asked him to write one sentence everyday (mechanics). He wrote "I hate this" rotating with "This is boring" for about a week. I stopped asking him to write. Instead, he began to read voraciously.

What writing he did was in thank you notes to relatives for gifts. These notes were written with my help. I would often answer the question "How do you spell such and such a word?" with a question of my own "How do you think it is spelled?" until I was told that this was not an acceptable answer. Josh told me that when he asked it didn't mean that he hadn't thought of how the word was spelled, he just wanted an answer. Now I answer the question about how to spell a word by giving the spelling if I know it. I had to bite my tongue at first to stop my first response of wanting to ask how the person thinks it is spelled. I remind myself that my children want an impersonal and immediate response like a word processor's spell check function.

I encouraged my children to tell me stories when they were very young. I wrote them down as they told them to me. As they grew older they continued to tell me stories. I was their scribe and recorded these stories in print. They made many books to give to their father on his birthday using a story they told me and then illustrating it.

These books are treasures. We enjoy looking at them and reading through them. Some of them were written and typed using invented spelling. Even the author now has a difficult time reading what was written, although I can often puzzle it out. As I read through these books of invented spelling, I remember each child at that age and how differently they each thought and wrote down (encoded) sounds.

Josh developed a very good grasp of composition from all the reading he did. He has a great ear for an authentic "voice" and can create characters with authentic voices in his writing, which is self-generated. I have never been involved in correcting or proofreading this writing. However, when he writes letters, promotional material, or other things for his work as a professional harpist, he consults with me just as I consult with him about most of my written work. We value and trust each other's judgment.

Robin completed his first book - a fantasy novel - in 2000 when he was 17 years old. He brings the reader into the world he's created instantly. I am still stunned by his talent. I am stunned because until Feb. of 2000, I hadn't read anything Robin had written for years. He asked me to help him tighten up the mechanics in his manuscript. It took just a few minutes of conversation to clarify some of these things. He's been editing his manuscript both for the mechanics and tightening up the writing for the last few months, part of the process before sending his manuscript to publishers. He's at work on the second book of this trilogy and has other books beyond this trilogy in mind as well.

Holly enjoys writing. She used to write lists of her dolls' names, their ages, their birth dates and phone numbers. She wrote notes from one doll to another. She enjoyed writing things when she was young and had a pen pal. She, more than her brothers, learned to read and write at the same time. She generated more spontaneous writing as she was learning to read than her brothers did. She's more oriented to verbal expression.

Let me digress here just momentarily to address the differences between my sons and daughter. My boys are oriented to building things, keeping statistics, playing games, observing patterns, etc. My daughter, while she has done these things, has always been more interested in relationships between people and playing family type games. This difference is very striking. I have wanted to believe at various times in my life that men and women are not different because frequently being a woman has meant being less.

I am so glad to see the beginning of a resurgence of appreciation for the strengths that women have traditionally expressed. I see acknowledgment here and there that we need to change the focus we have had in our world on male values as the only true values - i.e., thought divorced from feeling. A book that I found fascinating, *Brain Sex, The Real Difference Between Men and Women* by Anne Moir, Ph.D. and David Jessel, discusses the physiological differences between male and female brains. This information can be used to help us understand how to work with the differences that exist between men and women rather than blame each other for the differences and value one above the other.

Working with your children at home, you will notice differences. Some of these differences are related to personality, others are related to gender. Becoming more informed about the different ways men and women process information and events helps you to be more effective when you are helping your children learn how to write.

One of the ways that my children enjoyed learning about the parts of speech was through playing games of *Mad Lib*. These are games that consist of stories with blanks. Before reading the story, the players complete the list of words asked for, such as a singular noun, a verb, etc.   We did this in a group and asked each other in turn to give a noun, verb, adjective, adverb, etc. as was requested. We then filled in all the blanks and read the story using the words we had chosen. It can be quite a funny and painless way to help your children learn about the parts of speech. *Mad Libs* come with different themes and can be found in book and toy stores.

Now that personal computers and word processors are so readily available, helping your child learn how to use a keyboard efficiently is more than likely more beneficial than worrying about perfecting cursive hand writing.   John Holt, in his book *Learning All The Time* published posthumously, suggests that printing is faster than cursive writing. (Cursive writing is based on copperplate writing done by scribes.) We have done some time trials to see if his theory holds true. It is true for some members of our family and not for others.

I think it is important to realize that while you can help a child gain mastery of the physical skills of writing, knowing how to write doesn't mean that a child will chose to write. He may not have anything he wants to say. Helping a child learn to express himself is the other part of learning to write. Some children may find that words are not the form of choice for their expression. Instrumental music, art, movement, or song may suit them better than words.

Because I didn't want my children to feel that I was judging the validity of their work when they wrote things, I tried to remember not to correct their writing unless they asked. It was a struggle at first. I would never have considered changing a child's painting to make it look "right," why did I think I needed to change a child's writing? I would offer my help to correct spelling or add punctuation. Sometimes, I was taken up on my offer, often not.

In school, children are asked to do a lot of writing. I was concerned at various times when my children were young that they had not written very much. They spent a lot of time talking with me, each other, their friends, and their father. They recorded stories they made up on a tape recorder. They found ways of expressing themselves that felt comfortable to them. They knew how to form letters, both printed and cursive, and learned to use word processing programs. They did not chose to express themselves in writing very often when they were younger. I reminded myself frequently that most adults do not express themselves in writing very often. It is usually done verbally or if written, in journal form that is not for public consumption.

I like to see myself as a resource person for my children about writing - helping them with the rules of grammar, spelling, etc. - the way a librarian is a resource person for books. The librarian does not feel obliged to criticize or condemn a library patron for not knowing the Dewey decimal system. Instead, a librarian's function is to help a library patron find what it is he or she is looking for.

As well as writing stories, my children wrote some poems using techniques that my husband uses in his classroom. I showed my children how to write a poem using these techniques so that they could use them again if they so desired. None of the boys have chosen poetry as a regular form of self-generated expression finding other forms of expression more interesting: music, stories, drawing, and painting. Holly liked to make up poems. She didn't always write them down, instead she chanted them to herself.

I enjoyed the times we spent together writing poems because I like writing poems. I have a hard time accepting that what I write is poetry - "Can it really be poetry if I have written it and it can be understood?" Too much criticism of my writing by my teachers and too much time spent analyzing other poets when I was in high school and university made me very hesitant to call anything I write poetry. Doing this work with my children helped me be less critical of the poems I've written.

Young children seem to me to be natural poets. Their way of viewing the world is still so new. Each rain fall or summer breeze is different and experienced with a freshness and innocence that is delightful. Sometimes, they express their experience in words. Take time to write these expressions down when you can.

Following are two forms that you might find useful when you want to start writing a poem with your child.

Here's an example written by Robin when he was 8 years old about his rabbit Thumper. Start with a topic like a pet or favorite animal.

State it's name   **Thumper**
Then, it's color   **Gray, white, and black**
Describe it's size   **Medium size**
Describe where the animal lives...
                  He lives in a cage.
Describe what the animal eats...
                  He eats bananas, grass, and dandelions.
Describe the way it looks...
                  The way he looks is nice and cute.
Add a wish if you like...
                  I hope I'll have him as long as I live.

Another form that is fun to use is to put the letters of an animal's name on each line and start that line with that letter, an acrostic. Here are two examples by Noah, written when he was 10 years old:

Over the
Woods silently
Looking for mice.

Mostly scampering
Often found in the woods
Usually up at night
Sometimes stopping, sniffing
Eating flowers and seeds.

I liked helping my children write poems. I found it intriguing to read their poetry. It gave me a new glimpse into the way they perceive the world. Here are two poems that Josh wrote. The first he wrote when he was 12 years old using an acrostic format, the second, a self-generated poem, when he was 14 years old.

Crows calling, flapping around,
Riding on air, hopping on ground.
Only the raven matches his black.
With wings outspread, he flies.

Baseball

Baseball -
timeless,
unclockable,
never over till the last out
rich with tradition
filled with names like
Babe
Big Train
The Splendid Splinter
moments from the past
living on in memory
today it's different
yet the same.

My children were willing to write poems because they are short and can be rewritten easily, making corrections to cursive writing, grammar, and spelling easy to do.

In conclusion, writing consists of two parts: the mechanical side - letters, spelling, grammar, etc. - and the content. When you are helping your child learn to write, remember that it is the content, the message that is important. The mechanical side will come with time as long as a child is supported in his efforts. Give your child room to play around with words, writing styles, invented spelling and wait until asked to correct the mechanical side of the writing. Whenever possible be a scribe for your child so that he or she can see his or her stories written down. Help make the transition from verbal communication to written communication a gentle one, filled with encouragement.

CHAPTER 5
Mathematics

When Josh was 3 years old, he asked me many questions about how numbers worked and fit together, especially at bed time. He would fall asleep thinking about mathematical patterns. He was fascinated by numbers. He had a very mathematical mind.

Each of my children when they were toddlers enjoyed counting as we put cookies on a cookie sheet or as we cut a cake into pieces. They enjoyed having their fingers and toes counted or counting as we walked up and down the stairs. These activities and others like them are part of "math readiness."

Math readiness may not be something you thought about before. But, just as reading readiness is important, i.e., exposing children to stories, the printed page, words, etc., so is math readiness. In order for a child to understand about numbers and how they work, he or she needs to have had many experiences with numbers and number concepts.

Before you can help your child do the basics in mathematics - adding, subtracting, multiplying, and dividing - your child has to have an understanding of the one-to-one correspondence of numbers. Your child needs to know that 3 is 3 today, tomorrow, next week, and yesterday and that 3 is 3 whether the 3 objects are grouped close together or spread far apart.

John Holt in his book *How Children Fail* discusses the struggle that so many of the children he taught had with basic arithmetic. He described the panic that he saw in those children's faces when they would do arithmetic. They panicked because what happened during addition, subtraction, multiplication, or division seemed totally arbitrary, unpredictable, and confusing. They had no understanding of the one to one correspondence of numbers or the reliability of numbers.

Manipulative play with real objects is vital to develop an understanding of the predictability and reliability of numbers. Playing with things like Lego pieces, wooden blocks, beads, pennies, dolls, teddy bears, pine cones, rocks, sticks, etc. gives a child first hand experience that the 3 rocks he had yesterday are still 3 rocks today. A child needs to have many experiences like this in order to understand what the number "3" represents.

This repetitive experience during play is a developmental step that parents can encourage by giving children time and space to play in, things to play with, and a vocabulary of words to use. It is a developmental step that cannot be short-circuited and just taught – it must be learned and experienced by the child many times over.

Children who do not have an understanding of the one-to-one correspondence of numbers cannot add or subtract. They have no experience with the reliability of numbers and will often feel that there is a trick involved. If they could just learn the trick, then it would all be magically solved. The magic trick is to have a solid understanding of the one-to one correspondence of numbers.

With this solid understanding of the one to one correspondence of numbers (3 is 3 is 3 no matter how far apart or close together) and the reliability of numbers (3 is 3 is 3 whether it is today or tomorrow), addition, subtraction, multiplication, and division can be learned. A problem that is solved today (5+3=8) will have the same solution tomorrow. It is solid and predictable.

As well as manipulative play, it helps to give your child a vocabulary for arithmetic. Let me give you an example of how a simple conversation regarding cookies can help increase a child's understanding and mathematical vocabulary. Let us suppose that a 3 year old has 5 cookies. He eats 3 of the cookies and has 2 left. I describe the situation mathematically, "You had 5 cookies, then you ate 3 and now you've only got 2 left." If there were more cookies and my child was hungry, I'd offer more saying, "Here are 2 more cookies to add to the 2 you have left. That makes 4." If this is casually done, then over time a child develops a vocabulary to use. He observes numbers and their properties while he plays. Now that doesn't mean a child will necessarily talk about these concepts, but he will incorporate the vocabulary and use it to describe what he observes as he plays. All of this takes place almost subconsciously and most of the time internally although toddlers who have heard numbers will begin to count - "1,2,4,8,3, 10".

One of the ways to incorporate play with numbers into your daily life is to use finger plays like this one.

Here is the beehive. (hand closed in a fist)

Where are the bees? (look at the fist)

Hiding where nobody sees. (look around the fist)

Here they come creeping out of their hive (slowly lift up each finger)

One, Two Three, Four, Five (each finger is extended as you count)

Bzzz (make your hand fly around)

from *This Little Puffin* by Elizabeth Matterson, a great finger play resource!

Before starting any formal arithmetic work, I encourage you to observe your children to determine their understanding of numbers. Find out through observation if they have a solid grasp of the one to one correspondence of numbers. If your child is under the age of 5 or 6, begin to introduce the vocabulary of arithmetic, if you have not already done so. "Let's count how many apples we have left in the fruit bowl. Now let's subtract the 8 we need for a pie. Let's count how many we have left?" Describing your activities like this may take practice if it is not part of your normal vocabulary, but it is worth the effort.

If your child is older, you can still introduce the vocabulary of arithmetic, but it may seem a little forced. Mathematics is a way of describing and defining the events that take place in our lives. Just as I gave my children the names for objects and their colors, I gave my children names for the process of addition, subtraction, multiplying or dividing. It wasn't a formal lesson, just a part of everyday life.

As well as vocabulary, I provided opportunities for us to play with mathematical concepts. One of the activities my children enjoyed was stacking up pennies to see how high the stack was for a nickel, dime, quarter or dollar. We spent many hours playing with these pennies when each child was between 3-6 years old. They enjoyed it. While we played, I would make comparisons and encourage them to tell me about the differences they noticed in the various stacks of coins they made. It was a very satisfying way to see how numbers worked and the relationship of pennies to nickels, dimes, and quarters. This was all done at a very slow and relaxed pace while we sat on the floor. By the time the boys were 6 years old, they could easily determine if they could afford to buy a toy that they wanted. They did this figuring in their heads.

When Holly and I played with coins, she would group them into family units. She didn't show the same interest in knowing how much things cost as her brothers did until she was older. When her brothers would try to answer a number problem they often thought in terms of pennies or coins. Holly found it easier to answer if I described the problem in terms of families of animals or teddy bears. For example I would say "There's a family of 5 cats - a mommy, daddy, and 3 sisters. Two of the sister cats go off into the bushes to explore. How many cats are left?" Just as when you help your child learn to read you use material that fits his or her thought patterns, you look for ways to present number information in ways that appeal to your child. Cookies were a favorite way for everyone in our house to learn about adding, subtracting, and division.

Much of our arithmetic has been done through the games we play. One mental math game we enjoyed was to give each person who wanted to play a number question, for example "How much is 3+5?" as we rode in the car to the grocery store or sat around the kitchen table after supper. Each member of the family who wanted to play would ask someone else a number question in turn. The only rule was that the person asking the question had to know the answer to his or her own question. My husband and I tailored our questions so that each child could answer the question.

I always found it amazing to see how quickly even a younger

child grasped some of the basics of arithmetic and wanted to participate. At age 4, each of our children could do simple division problems in his or her head. If we have 2 cookies and 4 children, how many cookies does each child get? As the children mastered addition and subtraction of numbers to 10, the questions in our game became more difficult. They no longer needed to refer to actual objects (like their fingers) to solve the problem, they had a mental grasp of what each number stood for.

This number game and other games such as card games as well as various discussions of numbers and how they worked were not "lessons," they were a part of our family's daily life. This way of studying mathematics may seem haphazard yet my children developed an understanding of numbers and how they fit together without much trouble and at a fairly early age. They learned these things as they played.

I didn't start doing written math with my children until they were about 7½-8 years old. They were fascinated by the workbooks that they saw in our local K-Mart. They were eager to do the exercises in workbooks like *The Golden Step Ahead Books*. They would work intensely for a few days, finishing one and sometimes two workbooks. Then their interest would wane. Some of my children enjoyed doing each problem in the workbooks, others did one or two, figured out what they were supposed to do, weren't interested in doing more and then went on to the next page. Months passed before they showed another flurry of interest. These workbooks gave me an idea of what each child knew how to do and provided an opportunity for me to help them learn some of the skills they wanted to learn. Once they learned a new skill and practised it enough that they understood the procedure and could do it easily, they weren't interested in doing more problems.

By the time I was 8 years old, I had memorized the multiplication tables up to 12. I was concerned that Josh did not have this information memorized when he became 8 years old. I had to reassess my assumption that one must learn these tables by age 8 or else. (I am not sure what the "or else" was. I have never known just what the "or else" is. I have always assumed it to mean that some sort of catastrophe will befall one, but so far I haven't noticed that any of these catastrophes have happened.) I came to the realization that memorizing the multiplication tables did not mean understanding multiplication. At age 8, Josh's grasp of how numbers worked and the patterns they made was much more extensive than my own at age 8. He eventually learned the multiplication tables in the process of playing the games programmed into a Snoopy Calculator that we had.

One of the things I used to help my children learn multiplication was to write out the times table on a piece of graph paper. This can then be used as a reference. When Holly was 10, she decided to make a times table like this. I was making peach jam and thinking and measuring and she was busily working at the kitchen table asking me questions. She worked along happily; I made jam happily. I thought about how often my children ask me to help them learn something while I am in the middle of doing something I can't stop.

Holly made some very astute observations about the pattern of the numbers as she filled in the squares. She asked me a few times if her multiplication was correct and I found myself answering yes, knowing it wasn't quite right but at the same time counting out spoonfuls of pectin and not being able to count and multiply at the same time. As soon as I didn't need to concentrate so hard on what I was doing, I'd ask her to ask me again what she had just asked me and we corrected my errors.

This example epitomizes much of our homeschooling. It rarely happened that I sat down and "taught" my child something. My children often asked a question and were ready to absorb the answer during the "in between" times or the times when I was thinking about something else or concentrating on something. This can either drive you quite crazy or it can make you laugh. I usually laughed.

When the boys (at ages 11-12) were ready to learn long division, we worked together for about 15 minutes and then they had it figured out. They already understood multiplication. They had done lots of division problems in their heads. While learning to do division on paper was new, they were already familiar with division having done it mentally so often.

Learning the skills of how to solve arithmetic problems often requires lengthy explanations. One of the benefits of homeschooling is that you can take the time to answer a child's questions and ensure that he or she understands. Let me give you an example of what I mean. My brother, who designs and builds both hardware and software for computers, was told when he was 11 years old and in grade 5 that he was not very capable in math because he consistently had wrong answers by one digit to subtraction problems, i.e., 19-11=7. He tried to explain to his teacher that he needed to know where to start from when subtracting. She did not understand what he was trying to say and just told him that he needed to memorize the facts. She accused him of not studying because he kept getting the wrong answers. This teacher had no idea what my brother was asking. He probably didn't have the vocabulary to explain it as clearly as he could when he told me this story as an adult. His teacher told him that he was being difficult. She didn't have the time to discover just what he was trying to ask her.

These sorts of questions have come up in our family when a child asks just how many days it is until a birthday or Christmas. Different people in the family give different answers. Each answer is correct, but it's very confusing. We then spend time defining just what is being asked. Do you want to know how many sleeps it is, or how many days between today and the special day, or how many days it is from today not including today until the special day, etc.?

We have also had discussions about what is being asked in a problem such as 19-11=? Are we counting how many are left after you take 11 from 19? Then it would be 8. Are we asking how many numbers there are between 19 and 11? Then it would be 7. Are we counting how many numbers between and including the numbers 19 and 11? Then the answer would be 9. I explained to my children that the problem 19-11= means how many are left after you take away 11.

I had not anticipated these mathematical discussions. I thought I would just show my children how to add, subtract, etc. without any discussion. I never realized how interesting mathematics could be and that what had seemed to me to be a simple problem could be so complicated. These discussions were an introduction to logic and defining terms and helped me to carefully explain what I wanted when we did arithmetic problems together.

If you are uncertain about just how much your child would be expected to know about arithmetic at a given age if she were going to school, you could consult a math text book or work book appropriate for your child's age.   However, keep in mind that like with reading, children mature at different rates in their ability to understand math. You can't force understanding. You can encourage it and support it's development by providing what I have already mentioned – time to play and things to play with as well as words, a vocabulary, to use to describe mathematical activities.

As well as math textbooks borrowed from your local school, you might find the series of books by Marilyn Burns *Math for Smarty Pants*, *The I Hate Mathematics! Book*, and *The Book of Think* helpful. My husband, Larry, uses some of the exercises in these books in his classroom. For older homeschoolers (12 and up), try looking through *Stein's Refresher Mathematics* or *Arithmetic Made Simple* by A.T. Sperling and Samuel D. Levison.   Both of these books are easy to understand and cover the math needed through high school. You may want to check your library for copies to see if the format suits you.   You may also find these books a helpful resource for you to use rather than for your child. Some people find it reassuring to use a math textbook as a guide. Keep in mind that your child may skip from one thing to another, and that the order in a textbook is somewhat arbitrary.

I enjoyed paging through three math textbooks by Harold Jacobs *Mathematics A Human Endeavor*, *Algebra*, and *Geometry* published by W.H. Freeman and Company, 660 Market Street, San Francisco, California 94104. I like Jacob's approach. His textbooks are filled with cartoons, and he explains things clearly. The answers to many of the problems are listed in the back of the book which is helpful. The teacher's edition has interesting examples that expands the material presented in the student textbook. While I have looked through these books and enjoyed them, my boys have not shown a great deal of interest. When they were younger, their math tended to be related to roll playing games that used dice, logic puzzles, games, design, or how much money they had to buy a certain toy or game they wanted. I am sure that should they need to know any higher mathematics in the future, they'll have no trouble learning what they need to know.

If you are uncertain of your ability to teach mathematics to your child, remember textbooks are designed to teach. You don't already need to know the material before starting. If you find that you and your child get stuck, reach out to others for help. It is OK to ask for help. It models for your children that when you don't understand something or need more information, you turn to other resources to find the answer or help needed. A great lifelong skill to acquire.

If you are uncertain, you may want to take a basic math refresher course. You might also want to consider that there is nothing as effective in helping you to learn something than teaching it to someone else. You can start simply with basic addition with your child while you bake cookies or as you count pennies. You don't need to worry when your child is young how you will ever manage to teach her algebra. As you work with your child in a casual and relaxed way to explore the world of numbers, you may find that your confidence increases so that by the time your child is older and ready to tackle algebra you are, too.

If you find that rather than getting excited by exploring the world of mathematics, you want to run and hide because you are uncertain about your abilities, and wonder if you can still homeschool if you feel like this, you do have alternatives other than sending your child to school. You can find someone who is willing to tutor your child in this subject. Being a homeschooling mother doesn't mean you have to do everything yourself.

I asked Josh to help Robin review and learn the skills necessary to be able to do the problems on the Gauss Math Tests (University of Waterloo, ON Canada) from past years. Josh was more than happy to do this. Robin was willing to learn these skills from Josh. He is used to Josh helping him learn how to play various games. That is how they both approached this task - as a game.

Mathematics is not just numbers. Logic and deduction are part of it. The books about Encyclopedia Brown by Donald Sobol are great read aloud short problem stories that can be fun for children to think about and try to solve. These books are about a 10 year old detective and the problems he solves in his small hometown. Martin Gardner, who wrote for Scientific American, has written numerous books about logical thinking that may appeal to an older child, see the bibliography. (I mentioned his book *aha! Insight* in the chapter about reading.)

Another book that you might find fun to try is *The Calculator Game Book for Kids of All Ages* by Arlene Hartman. It has a number of games a child can play with a calculator.

As well as arithmetic, mathematics consists of spatial relationships. Puzzles, origami, making quilt squares, designing buildings, drawing, cutting out paper dolls, etc. all involve spatial relationships. As a child plays with puzzles or building blocks, he begins to develop an understanding of how things fit together, he develops a sense of the relationship of one thing with another. Compass constructions and mazes also involve an understanding of spatial relationships and can be fun for children. (See the bibliography for recommended books.)

Playing games has been one of the most consistent forms of mathematics we have done. Board and card games can be an almost invisible way for a child to learn and understand numerical sequence, addition, and subtraction. Playing games develops the ability to think logically and sequentially, a necessary part of mathematics. As you and your child have fun, you help your child improve his or her math skills. I have listed a number of games that we enjoyed below. The board games I list are often available at thrift shops at much more reasonable prices than buying them new. (We enjoy looking for games at places like Goodwill or Value Village because we can then afford to try games we are not sure about.)

I have not listed any computer games because until quite recently we did not have a computer and therefore, I am not knowledgeable about these games. My concern about computer games is that it isolates a child. Young children especially need to have interactions with real, live people and play games within the context of a relationship rather than sitting in front of a monitor. A computer also does not give a child real things to manipulate and count. It works in symbols and as numbers are also symbols for real objects, it can be a very confusing way for a child to acquire an understanding of how numbers work. There are no real objects to hold, feel, and move about.

The Atlantic Monthly July 97 issue had an article "The Computer Delusion" by Todd Oppenheimer that discusses computers at length and how they have not significantly improved teaching or learning. There is other information about computers in the classroom that you may find interesting. Look in the bibliography of this chapter.

Besides helping my children with many basic mathematical skills, playing games also gave them experience in negotiating with others and an appreciation of the need for structure and rules. They have discovered that if we do not have the rules established before playing a game, arguments become the activity instead of the game we intended to play. Even when rules are established, there is room for interpretation as, for example, the call of balls and strikes in baseball by the umpire. Games can be a great forum for learning the art of consensus.

When all my children were little they enjoyed games like Red Light Green Light, Mother May I, and Pussy In The Corner. These were simple games with easy to understand rules. Everyone had a chance to participate. As Josh and Noah grew older, we started to play more complicated games that required more skill - such as card games. These games were on the whole competitive. We did try various commercially produced cooperative games, but Josh and Noah found them very boring after the age of 5. Holly and Robin enjoyed cooperative games longer. When Holly and I played together, she often turned a competitive card game into a cooperative one.

I struggled with my conscience about teaching my children competitive games. I didn't like setting up someone to lose. I found it hard to help the loser deal with his emotions and would often suggest that we play something else. Josh and Noah wanted to keep playing competitive games and persisted in spite of the tears and frustrations. As they grew older they acquired more game playing skills and gradually learned to cope with their feelings about losing.

Robin began playing board and card games with his older brothers when he was about 4½ years old. He told me that he never expected to win when he was younger, he just enjoyed being included. As Robin grew older winning became more important so we set up handicaps for some games according to the player's age and skill level to compensate for varying age and skill levels. As his skill level increased, Robin no longer found handicaps necessary. It's something you may wish to consider doing in your family.

At the end of this chapter, I have listed a number of games we have enjoyed as a family. I hope you find some that your family will enjoy. Some people thrive on certain kinds of games that others find boring. Some thrive on competitive games, some don't. Try some of these games and observe your child to see which ones bring pleasure.

When choosing games from this list, please remember that the age range is an approximation. What will work for a 5 year old who is third in a family may not work for a 5 year old who is first and vice versa. Children who have watched older siblings play games already have a framework for how to play a game.

Learning the skills involved in playing games is something that takes time. Being able to wait one's turn, being able to count, being able to match colors are all skills that playing games rely on and strengthen. Part of the fun of being a homeschooling parent is that the time you spend playing games with your children is part of their education.

I hope that this chapter has given you an idea of where to start with mathematics and has given you enough information to feel comfortable about helping your child learn about mathematics. As you work with your child, remember to work from a place of patience and calm. If whatever you are doing isn't working and you and/or your child become frustrated, change activities. There's a book called *Always Change a Losing Game* which says it all in the title. Have fun! Enjoy the fascinating world of mathematics. It is a much bigger world than one limited to arithmetic. Explore spatial relationships with puzzles, origami, sewing patchwork quilts, building with blocks, decorating a cake, or other things. Play games like poker or gin rummy and learn about predictability and probability as you play. Once you start thinking about it, you will notice opportunities to see the world in a mathematical way. Seed pods in the garden become representatives of geometric shapes. Baking cookies becomes an exercise in times tables and addition, etc. Like a child who is starting to read and suddenly notices all the words everywhere he looks, you will see the many ways mathematics are a part of your life.

One of the great things about doing math informally by using games, doing puzzles, or observing nature is that you can show a child that it is OK to make mistakes (as in choosing the wrong puzzle piece and then finding it doesn't work). It has made mathematics so much more pleasurable and exciting for me. It tickled my fancy to think that when I did a puzzle with my children we were doing math. Mathematics is so much more than computation. It is way of perceiving and defining the world. And now for that list of games.

Prop-less Games
Games that can be played almost anywhere

Animal, Vegetable, Mineral from age 3-4 up. This was a favorite guessing game in our family when the children were young and came with me to do errands. One person chooses an object and decides its category - animal, vegetable, mineral. The others ask a question with a 'yes' or 'no' answer, one question at a time in turn. Eventually the other players discover what the object is or the other players give up. A new player chooses an object and the game starts again.

For younger children, it may be easier to first start with just one category such as animals and define clearly just what will fit into the category of animal. This game lends itself to great discussions about what things are made of "In what category is a Lego block?" and can be a fun way to pass the time as you are driving around doing errands. Limit the numbers of players to keep everyone involved. A larger group means that everyone has to wait too long for a turn. We found 4-5 players were as much as we could manage.

Charades Ages 5 and up. One of my favorite games. We play in teams of two or three with each team choosing a book, song, or movie title to act out. The teams go to separate parts of the house to discuss how they will act out the title. When everyone is ready, we all go into the same room and start.

Each team presents the charade they have chosen. The other

teams all try to guess what the title is. No score is kept. No points are won or lost. We just have a lot of fun and laughter. It's a great game for a mixed age group. Even young children can be included as part of a team and can act out the charade with the other team members. Having a mixed age team also has the advantage of helping a younger child learn how to act out words, what strategies to use when words rhyme or sound like other words, etc.

I Spy Ages 3 and up. "I spy with my little eye, something that is green." The other players ask questions with "Yes" or "No" answers until the object is found. I found it interesting to observe my children develop systematic approaches to locate the object in a room by asking questions that eliminated parts of the room as well as asking questions that eliminate certain categories of objects. This game and others like it that rely on answers to yes or no questions help children develop problem solving techniques.

As we played these games, my major goal was fun while keeping my children happily occupied. Yet these games were invaluable in developing some of the basic skills required to do mathematical problems. The advantage of playing these sorts of games in a mixed age group is that older players can model problem solving skills for younger ones. We played these sorts of games for more hours than I can count. No wonder my children think of problem solving as an interesting challenge.

Mother May I? Ages 2 and up. I remember playing this game frequently with Noah and Josh when they were 1½ and 3½ years old. They thought it was a great game. One player is the *mother*. *Mother* stands in a certain spot. (We played in a hallway with *mother* at one end.) The other players line up at a defined distance from *mother*. *Mother* then calls each player by name, in turn, and tells them that s/he can take a certain number of steps. "Noah, you may take 4 steps." This player must then ask "Mother may I?" *Mother* then replies with "Yes, you may." or "No, you may not. You may take 2 steps (or whatever number chosen)."

If the answer is 'yes,' the player moves the numbers of steps *mother* has said. If the answer is 'no,' the player again asks "Mother, may I?"

in response to the number of steps *Mother* has said. If a player does not ask "Mother may I?" and begins to move the 4 steps suggested, s/he must go back to the beginning and start again. Eventually one player will reach *Mother*, tag her and that player now becomes *Mother* and the whole game starts over again.

This game can be varied by being creative with the kind of steps *Mother* asks the children to take - baby steps, giant steps, whirly twirly steps, hops, etc. It can be very powerful for a small child to be in charge and have everyone moving just the way s/he wants. This game as well as Pussy in the Corner and Red Light Green Light can help a young child begin to understand the framework of how a game is played. It is a game that is physical and fairly simple. Adult participation (or that of an older child) ensures that the game does not lead to arguments about the sizes of the steps. My children enjoyed this game until they were about 8 years old. After that, it lost it's appeal. As I was growing up, I remember playing this game at school during lunch and recess through 6th grade. We played outside on a large paved area the size of a basketball court with about 15-20 girls.

Pussy In The Corner   Age 3 and up. We started playing this game after reading The Little House Books by Laura Ingalls Wilder. You need room to play this game.   Find a space that has one less "corner" than player. (You don't have to have actual corners, you can designate certain places in the room as a corner.) One player is in the middle and the other players are all in their corners. The person in the middle shouts out "Pussy wants a corner." All the players have to move to a new corner. The person in the middle runs to a corner as well. The player left over goes to the center and begins the game anew by shouting "Pussy wants a corner." It's a great way to burn off energy during inclement weather. Make sure the place you are playing is safe for running. Because the game moves so fast, everyone gets a chance to both be in a corner and be in the middle fairly often.

Guess Who?   Ages 4-5 and up. Another yes and no question game. This time one person chooses a character from a book and the other players try to guess who it is by asking yes or no questions. The only rule we established was that the character had to be from a book that was familiar to all the players.

Red Light Green Light Ages 4 and up. One person is *It* and stands in a particular spot. The other players line up at least 10 feet away. *It* turns around, away from the other players so that his/her back is to the other players and calls out "Green Light." The other players move toward *It* and try to tag *It*. *It* can say "Red Light" at anytime and turn around to face the other players. Any player seen moving by *It* is told to go back to the starting line. *It* then turns around again and says "Green Light." When there is a mixed age group, make sure rules are established that specify that there is no pushing or shoving. An adult playing the game helps set the tone of having fun without anyone getting hurt.

Sardines Ages 2 and up. Sardines is a form of hide and seek where It hides. The other players find It, and then hide with It until everyone is hiding. The first person to find and hide with It becomes It for the next game. Fun to play both inside and outside. My children have enjoyed games of sardines and hide and seek since they were very small. Both of these games are good games to play with a mixed age group.

Board Games

Following is a list of some of the commercial board games our family has enjoyed. Some of these games may no longer be available new but can be found secondhand at garage sales or thrift shops. This list is only a beginning guide. I know there are lots more games out there for families to enjoy playing together.

Casino Yahtzee ages 7 and up. A game of chance using dice, up to 4 people can play at once.

Checkers, Chinese Checkers, Chess, Go ages 5 and up. We used handicaps for some of these games to balance the skill level between the players.

Clue A player needs to be able to read or have a partner who can read in order to play. Can be played by up to 6 players. A game that can develop logical reasoning, deductive thinking.

Conspiracy A player needs to be able to add and subtract numbers, write numbers down, and read in order to play or have a partner who can do these things. It is best played with at least 3 players, 4 is maximum. A game of double crossing spies where you, as a player, try to bring home a briefcase of important papers.

Max A cooperative game for ages 3-4 (with adult help) and up. It involves the players working together to get the little animals home before Max, the cat, catches them.

Scotland Yard ages 10 and up. Best played with only two players, otherwise it becomes a long and tedious game. Players use maps of the underground transit system and streets of London. One player is the detective, the other is the criminal.

Sleeping Grump A cooperative game for ages 4 and up with adult help. Players try to get the treasure before the giant wakes up.

Survive ages 5 and up. Up to 4 players. The players attempt to get off an island that is sinking before a volcano explodes. Could be played cooperatively.

Card Games

Here are some of the card games that we've enjoyed that use a regular card deck. I have listed approximate ages. Libraries carry numerous books about how to play card games, so I won't duplicate that information here. Grandparents or other older people can be a good resource for help to learn new card games. A cardboard box can serve as an effective screen so that a small child who cannot hold his or her cards in his or her hands can spread the cards out and no one else can see them.

Crazy Eights from 5 up

Cribbage from 6 up, need to be able to add up to fifteen

Euchre from 7 up

Hearts from 6 up - always a difficult game for me to play as I don't like giving someone the Queen of Spades to make them lose.

Kings in the Corner from 5 up. Can be played cooperatively.

Pig from 5-6 up

Poker from 6-7 up

Solitaire from 7 up

Spit from 8 up

The following is a list of card games we have enjoyed that use their own unique decks.

Beggars and Thieves from 7 up. A great game. If you find it, buy an extra set. Lots of fun and an easy way to learn about trump cards.

Phase 10 from 7 up. This game kept Holly happy for hours when she was 7 years old and her brothers were all sick. Can be played cooperatively by not keeping score and turning the cards face up.

Old Maid from 4-5 up. Simple and fun as long as children can cope with losing.

Uno from 4-5 up. A commercial version of Crazy Eights. Because the numbers are so big and the colors so easy to identify, it might be a good way to start playing with cards. Robin liked this game a lot when he was about 4 years old. We took out the "pick up 2 or 4 cards" and played with our cards face up in front of us so that we could help each other.

Wizard from 9 and up.

Noah's Lego bird 1989

CHAPTER 6
The Arts:
Music, Art, Dance, Drama, and Phys. Ed.

Although at first glance helping a child to learn to play an instrument, sing a song, draw a picture, or do a dance may not seem to be as important as learning to read, or do arithmetic, it is. The arts are important because they provide an avenue for expression, a way for a child to create or express his or her response to life, a way to give meaning to life. Children just naturally express themselves in creative ways. It is as natural to them as breathing. If we provide materials, space, lessons (when needed), and encouragement, our children will do the rest.

The arts are part of what make us human. When we listen to a piece of music, watch a play or movie, or attend a dance performance, we have a chance to explore our feelings in a safe setting. We can feel joy, sadness, awe, anger, fear, etc. We can identify with the actors or dancers and see some of our own feelings acted out and see the results of those feelings in action. A performance whether it is drama, dance, or music takes us out of our usual sphere of reference and gives us a new perspective exposing us to a larger view of the world. Visual art helps us to see something a little differently, to perhaps see a little more of the everyday world than we usually do. Art feeds our souls.

Children need to have a chance to create, perform, dance, or make music themselves. This can be at a very simple basic level as well as at a more complex and difficult level. At the same time, it's important for children to see or hear other people perform. If it's at all possible, take your children to age appropriate live arts events. They are a wonderful way to enlarge a child's world and often stimulates their own play.

Before I go any further, I'd like to take a little detour. In this chapter about the arts, I will mention my children and their accomplishments in the fields of music and art. As you read this chapter, please keep in mind that what is important is exposing your child to various artistic modes of expression not whether or not he or she becomes a "star."

I do not want you to feel as I did when I read some books about homeschooling years ago when my children were very young. I read about a 12 year old child who knit incredible sweaters for her family for Christmas. I read about very musically talented children. After reading about these children, I felt deflated and rather hopeless. I remember wondering if I had the ability to help my children achieve some sort of expertise in a field of their choosing. I also felt doubtful that my children would show any sort of talent for anything in particular. I don't think that the authors intended to create feelings of inadequacy. Instead, I think that they were just sharing their delight in their children's abilities.

As you read this chapter, please keep in mind that the information I share about my children is meant to illustrate the points I am trying to make. My children's accomplishments in the arts are not intended to be used as a ruler to measure your child's abilities. Instead, I hope that it will inspire you to explore the arts with your child. Please keep in mind that a child can enjoy music, art, dance, etc. at whatever skill level suits the child. What's important is the enjoyment, the chance to express one's self. With that said, let's move on to music, as it is such a big part of our lives.

Music

When Josh and Noah were 4½ and 2½ years old, I spent many nights worrying about how they were ever going to learn music. We lived in a small rented house that didn't have enough room for a piano nor could we afford one. I was convinced by the little bit I knew about the Suzuki method of music instruction that if they didn't start then (and perhaps it was already too late for Josh, after all he was already 4½ years old!), they would never be able to play a musical instrument. I think I was so set on the piano because I had longed to play the piano as a child. Josh is now a professional harpist. He started harp lessons when he was 13½ years old.

So why did I get so worried? I didn't do enough critical thinking about the idea that a child has to start playing a musical instrument at age 3 or 4. The adage "a little knowledge is a dangerous thing" certainly fit me in this situation. I wanted the best for my children. The little bit I had read about the Suzuki method seemed at the time to be the best. I did not explore other ideas about music instruction nor did I take time to look at my own experience in learning to play an instrument. Instead, I worried. I worried for about 3 months, and then accepted our circumstances and moved on to other things. (I was pregnant with Robin, our third son, at the time.)

In the intervening years, I have had time to think about music in the early years. Exposure to music is what is important. While the Suzuki Method stresses learning to play an instrument at an early age (3 to 4 years old) as well as early exposure to music, I think early exposure to music is what is vital. Children of 3 and 4 years old do not have the eye hand coordination nor the mental development to progress very fast with a musical instrument. (There are exceptions of course.) Progress often comes more readily once a child reaches the age of 8-10. Josh started playing the harp when he was 13½ years old. Robin started to play the drums and marimba when he was 12 years old. It has not been a handicap for either of them to have started at these ages.

Marty's Method for music in the early years says that it's exposure to and the experience of music that's important. That means hearing it, singing it, moving to it, clapping to it, playing it on harmonicas, kazoos, slide whistles, drums, jars with popcorn and/or beans, etc. I wish I had known this when my oldest boys were little. I wish I could go back in time and give my younger self a picture of the present. What a relief it would have been for me to know that I didn't irreparably damage my children's ability to express themselves musically because we did not start Suzuki piano lessons when Josh was 4½ years old! We did follow my method of music, but I didn't know then that it would become a method!

Why is exposure to music in the early years important for children? Remember the "nomes" from Terry Pratchett's books that I mentioned in Chapter 1? It's hard to learn something or even imagine it exists if you have never had an experience of it. Just as we provide our children with experiences of language by reading stories and talking, we need to provide musical experiences for our children. The more music a child has had exposure to, the more familiar music will be, making it easier to learn to play music should a child choose to do so at a future date. Music has been a way that all people throughout time and in various places have expressed themselves. Music like poetry is for many children a "natural" language. Small children will sing as they play making up little tunes, especially if music has been a part of their daily lives.

The experience of listening to slow classical music has been shown to improve a person's ability to learn. "Learning improved by 24%, memory improved by 26% with the use of Baroque music" - Iowa State University. In the book *Superlearning*, authors Sheila Ostrander and Lynn Schroeder discuss this at great length with both scientific studies and anecdotal stories demonstrating the effects of listening to classical music at the largo tempo (approximately 60 beats per minute). Listening to this music has a calming effect as well.

You may have come from a home that did not have music or you may like a certain kind of music and know very little about any other kind. This may make you hesitant about presenting music to your children. You might be wondering just how to get started. I suggest that you start by singing to your babies. If it is too late for that, sing along with various recorded music for children as you and your children listen. Don't worry about your singing voice, just sing along. Many adults were told when they were children that they couldn't carry a tune. If this happened to you, sing with your child anyway. Your child has not received the same negative programming about your voice and efforts to sing that you did. Instead your child will be pleased that you are singing - it's fun when Mom sings along - and will join in with you.

My all time favorite children's singer is Raffi. He's a fine musician who exudes warmth, genuine caring, and fun. The musicians that accompany him are all excellent. His many recordings (*Singable Songs For the Very Young*; *More Singable Songs*; *Corner Grocery Store*; *Rise and Shine*; *Baby Beluga*; *One Light, One Sun*; *Raffi's Christmas Album*; *Everything Grows*; *Bananaphone*; *Raffi Radio*) are great to listen to and sing along with. I've been listening to him since 1979 and still enjoy each recording. He introduces different musical styles - jazz, country and western, rock and roll, classical, etc. using children's songs. For example, Raffi turns the song "Old MacDonald Had A Farm" into "Old MacDonald Had a Band" introducing various musical instruments in a delightful way.

Other singers we have enjoyed include Tom Chapin, Fred Penner, Tom Paxton, Malvina Reynolds, and The Travellers. I've just recently become aware of Jessica Harper - *A Wonderful Life*. She has a lovely voice and her recordings have a lot of upbeat songs. Rick Scott is a spokesperson for the Down's Syndrome Foundation. He has a song on his CD *Philharmonic Fool* "Angels Do" that he made into a video starring his granddaughter Mielle who has Down's syndrome. It's lovely. You can check his web site, www.rick-scott.com for more information.

The library can be a great resource for children's music. Borrowing cassettes or CDs from the library can help you find which musicians suit your taste or strike your fancy, and then you can purchase those recordings. Now that Josh has entered the recording world (*The Eclectic Harp* - a cassette - and *Josh Layne, A Harp Recital*, and *An Afternoon of Harp Music* - both CDs), I am more aware of how hard musicians work to produce their recordings. It seems only right that they should be paid for their recordings rather than having them copied.

My mom sang to me when I was little. I still remember the Dutch songs and some of the poems that she taught me. One of my favorite family memories took place when I was 18 years old. My mom, my brother, my sister and I drove to Washington, D.C. We were going to meet my mother's brother who had been sent there by the German TV station he worked for. We were going to see our grandmother, our Oma, for the first time in 10 years. I remember the songs we sang together, the harmonies we created together as we rode in the car. It was fun.

I sang a lot with my children as we drove around doing errands when they were little as well as singing with them at home. Sometimes we sang along to a cassette tape but just as often we'd sing by ourselves. As everyone grew older, we sang rounds. Holly in particular enjoyed singing with me as we went to the grocery store or did other errands. When she was a baby and toddler we sang in the car as a way to keep everyone busily occupied. As everyone grew older, the singing we did in the car was a way to express delight in singing.

Another way to expose your children to music is to listen to and enjoy music yourself. Josh became interested in learning to play the harp after listening to a lot of recorded Celtic harp music as he and his brothers and sister worked on a 1500 piece puzzle. My husband and I were going through a marriage crisis at the time, and both the puzzle and the music were calming for all of us. Out of that very stressful time came many positive results including Josh's interest in the harp. Everything fell into place - we found a harp for Josh and a wonderful teacher at the same time.

A child may express an interest in learning to play an instrument after listening to music as Josh did. Sometimes a child expresses a desire to play a certain instrument seemingly out of the blue. When Robin was 12 years old, he expressed an interest in learning to play the drums. We looked around for a percussion teacher and were lucky again to find another wonderful teacher. Robin enjoyed working with his teacher as much as his teacher enjoyed working with him. We bought a drum set from our 83 year old neighbor; and Robin began practicing. It took a while to get used to the drums after hearing harp music! A few months after Robin started the drums, he began to play mallet instruments. He now has a marimba. Robin likes all percussion instruments and happily practices many hours a day. When he was younger he played with Lego for many hours, now he plays his drums and marimba.

I wanted to learn to play the French horn as a child, but all the school system's French horns were taken. My mom suggested the oboe instead. I had lessons through the school band and orchestra program starting when I was 10 years old. I loved the sound of the oboe and enjoyed learning how to play it.

How can you help your child discover if he or she wants to play an instrument and if so, which one? Exposure to various instruments through recordings such as the ones I have mentioned as well as classical or other recordings like *The Orchestra* (available as a book and cassette or as a video) or the musical story *Peter and the Wolf* can help you and your child learn which instruments make which sounds.

Take your child to live performances. In some communities there are community orchestras or bands that offer concerts at relatively inexpensive cost, or there may be a professional orchestra in your community that offers special children's concert programs. If there is a university or college nearby with a music program, take advantage of their student recitals. They are usually free.

It's also fun to go to a music store and look at the various musical instruments, especially after listening to something like *The Orchestra*. And of course the library should have books about musical instruments with photos or other illustrations.

If your child expresses an interest in learning to play a musical instrument, finding a teacher may require some detective work on your part. If you are able to work with a your local elementary school, you may be able to be part of the school's music program and not have to pay for lessons. It is always worthwhile to explore this option. If this is not possible, or doesn't interest you, there are other places to look for music instruction for your child.

If you live in a city that has an orchestra, your city more than likely also has a music conservatory or similar institution where music is taught. Talk to people in music stores, ask members of orchestras or bands for names of teachers. Before signing on with any music teacher for any length of time agree to a trial of 2 lessons to see how this is going to work. Rent an instrument at first so that you and your child can see if this is an interest that your child wants to pursue. Check for special rental rates at the music stores in your area.

Holly expressed an interest in learning to play the trumpet when she was 9 years old. We rented a trumpet and found a teacher. Holly went to 2 lessons and then decided that this was not for her. We returned the trumpet and I let the teacher know that Holly would not be continuing her lessons.

The experience was a disappointment for Holly, as she really liked the sound of the trumpet. The teacher was a good trumpet player, but not necessarily the right teacher for Holly. Holly and I talked at length about looking for a different teacher, but she decided that she didn't like the trumpet enough to practice as long as she knew she would need to, to make progress. She decided to join a choir and sing instead.

I sat in on Holly's two trumpet lessons, which helped me clarify for her why she wasn't happy. Her teacher did not help her to see how much she had progressed in one week. Instead, the teacher focused on what Holly needed to correct and then added a few words of praise almost as an after thought. Knowing my daughter as I did, I knew that she had only heard the corrections and not the words of praise.

It took me a while to accept that it was OK to have allowed this experience to happen to my child. I reminded myself that it was short, and that my daughter was supported in her exploration of why she was not pleased by this experience. I reminded myself that it is only by trying different things that we can find out what will work, but I wished that it had been different. In hindsight, I wish that I had sat in on another child's lesson to get a better idea of this teacher's teaching style, or met her in person. A telephone conversation was not enough. However, even meeting with someone may not make clear how well this particular teacher and your child will work together. I realized, too, how much more I was effected by this than Holly was (related, I am sure, to my own experiences with music teachers).

The teachers I had during the seven years I played the oboe were mixed. I remember how terrified I was of making mistakes. No one ever told me that every musician makes mistakes. "It's what you do between the mistakes," as Pablo Casals said, "that counts."

It may take a while to find the right teacher for your child. The work you do to find a teacher who works well with your child is worth as much effort as you can give it. A good music teacher is worth his or her weight in gold. A music teacher who enjoys teaching and is a good musician is a joy and inspiration. I hope you will be as lucky as Josh and Robin have been. They both have excellent teachers.

One of the issues that concerns many parents when their child begins to learn a musical instrument is practice times. In order to learn how to play a musical instrument, a child needs to practice. The length of time a child practices everyday is not as important as practicing everyday. Fifteen minutes a day is adequate at the beginning. It is the everyday practice that builds skill and familiarity. It doesn't work to skip a few days and then practice 3 times as long. It's like building muscle strength, it takes place over time and can't happen all at once.

Encourage your child to practice by having a space available as well as your time available if your child wants your help. It may be helpful to discuss with your child when the practice will take place. Does your child want help to be reminded? Does your child want you to be there as he practices? Sorting out these things before hand makes this new learning activity something that you help your child with rather than something that comes between you.

Robin's self-discipline astounds me. When he started playing the drums, he practiced about an hour a day at first and worked his way up to 2½ hours a day. He continues to practice many hours a day on his drums and marimba. In order for him to take part in other activities, he has to rearrange his practice schedule and needs notification in advance. He does this because he loves it! All that practice has good results and he has made very rapid progress.

Robin had Josh as an example. He watched Josh progress from 30 minutes a day of practicing to 4½ hours a day as Josh learned more and more music. Robin has also watched Josh prepare for recitals and performances and looks forward to doing those himself. He's been lucky to have Josh as his live in model. To play the harp well requires lots of preparation time as it is one of the more difficult instruments to play. Robin expects that playing music well will take work. He does the work because he loves it.

I can remember my own excitement when I first got my oboe and began to learn to play. I practiced with a great deal of excitement and enthusiasm. Somewhere along the line my enthusiasm became tainted by fear. I needed help from my teachers to continue to feel enthusiastic through the difficulties of mastering the oboe. Instead, I was told about the many mistakes I made. The expectations were very high, and I never felt that I would be able to meet them. The only time I was aware that I had played well was when I hadn't made any mistakes and no one hassled me. I kept playing in spite of this lack of encouragement because I loved the oboe, I loved music, and I loved playing in an orchestra - making music with other people.

Josh's harp teacher, Kathryn Ely, has done a lot to help me become aware of the negative programming I received about my abilities as a musician. She is an inspiring teacher. Let me give you an example. A few years ago Josh was working on a piece that Zabaleta, a well-known harpist, had recorded. Kathryn asked Josh if Zabaleta played this section faster. Josh answered, "Yes." She encouraged Josh to play it faster - "If Zabaleta did it, so can you." I would have fallen off my chair if one of my music teachers had ever said that to me. I never felt that they were on my side. Instead, I thought that I would never be good enough to please them.

Learning the skills required - the technical skills to play an instrument - is hard work. It requires practice and dedication as well as enthusiasm. It is hard to practice and improve if a child works in an atmosphere that doesn't support the child's effort or recognizes the progress being made. If you notice that your child's initial enthusiasm wanes and you are nagging your child to practice, it may be time to review what is going on for your child. It may be that the amount of work involved in learning to play an instrument is more than your child bargained for; it may be that the teacher is not the right one for your child and your child feels discouraged; or it may be something else entirely. Help your child by supporting him or her to think about what may be causing the lack of enthusiasm to practice.

If your child no longer wants to play an instrument, then accept your child's decision and move on to another activity. This may be difficult to do because many of us have been taught that a child can't really make a decision about whether or not he likes an instrument until he's played it a while. I don't think this is true. Music comes from the heart. If a child's heart is not in it, if the heart does not sing, then the music can't come through. The work of learning to play an instrument is too hard to tackle if a child finds no joy in the process.

Two of my sons spend the better part of each day practicing their music. This is unusual. Homeschooling has allowed them time to explore their interest and given them time to practice but it did not create their talent or their love for their instruments. I would not like anyone to think that because a child is homeschooled he or she will become a professional musician, professional dancer, doctor, scientist, artist, or anything else. Instead, homeschooling can give children the time to pursue their interests in depth to discover what calls to them, what makes their hearts sing. The time that a homeschooling child has to pursue an interest can reveal talent but it can't create it.

People will often ask what my daughter does as her brothers all seem to have found their niche. She has begun to dance, so I often answer with that. Before she began to dance, I talked about how much she enjoys playing - with her pets, her toys, her brothers, and her friends. As a society we pay lip service to the idea that every person on the earth comes with special gifts, but we tend to recognize only outstanding gifts that fall in recognized categories like art, music, dance, drama, or sports. We are not willing to recognize talent for something like happiness, listening to others, being a warm-person, taking delight in a rainy day, etc.

It's important to remember that the uniqueness of your child may not fall into a recognized category. There's a woman I think of frequently when I think of our hero worship of "stars." This woman worked in my local post office when my children were young. She had a gift for creating peace. During pre-Christmas lineups, her talent for recognizing each person, making eye contact, and speaking calmly was a real treasure. When my turn would come, her warmth and good humor would fill my depleted reservoir of patience and I'd leave feeling so much better. I saw this happening to others in the line as well. Her gift doesn't fall into a recognized category nor would she be publicly acknowledged in any way, yet she made a difference to her customers. Ten years later I still think of her, thankful for our encounters.

One of the things I have already mentioned in this chapter is singing. Singing doesn't have to be formal, it can be just a natural outpouring of music. Children often hum or make up songs as they swing or play by themselves. From what I understand, it is better for a child to just sing until he or she has reached physical maturity at 13 or 14 years old before taking formal voice training. Churches often have children's choirs and communities may also have children's choirs. Sometimes schools are willing to include homeschoolers in their choirs. Again, detective work is needed to find just what will fit for your child if your child is interested in singing in a choir. If your child wants to sing and also wants to have lessons of some kind, encourage your child to try the piano or another musical instrument rather than having voice lessons. Learning to read music and how to play a keyboard instrument will be helpful for anyone who wants to sing.

Josh, Robin, and Noah playing recorders 1983

Dance - Physical Education

At our house, music and dancing have just naturally gone together. When we lived in that small house I mentioned at the beginning of this chapter, we used to dance to Raffi's music on cold winter days for our exercise, clapping our hands, singing along, and taking turns bouncing in rhythm on the Rebounder. When my children were small, we'd hold hands and dance, or one child at a time, they would dance in my arms. It was a great way to burn up energy and let off steam for all of us.

Just as it is important to sing to and with your child, it is important to move to music with your child. You don't have to be a great dancer or know particular steps, you just need to move to the music. Moving with your child to music encourages your child to do this on his or her own. Children are so physical. They dance with excitement or joy when something especially pleasant has happened.

You can use dance to encourage your child to express himself. I used to put on slow quiet classical music, and ask my children when they were between the ages of 1½-5 to pretend that they were seeds planted in the ground; then to imagine that they were sprouting and slowly reaching their roots down into the earth and their first leaves up into the sun. Depending on how much my children were enjoying this and how energetic they were, there would be rain, a gentle wind or a strong wind, sun, hail, etc. until the seed had turned into a tall tree. They enjoyed this tremendously. Dance moved into drama and then back again into dance. If you can play piano, it's a great instrument for accompaniment to a dramatic dance like this as you can vary the music to fit the activity - soothing for gentle rain, strident and loud for a hail storm. Sometimes my children would be the ones leading the dance and they played on the piano or a small tambourine making up music to suit the occasion, pounding hard for storms and more gently for sunshine.   This kind of musical dancing play was a great way to spend rainy days when we couldn't go outside.

Opportunities for children to learn to dance seem to be available in most communities. One way to explore just what is available in your community and to get an overview of what a particular dance school or teacher offers is to attend an end of the year recital. These usually occur in the spring. In the fall, dance schools sometimes hold open houses where you can also learn about the types of dance instruction offered. Don't limit yourself to ballet - there are lots of different kinds of dance: clogging, folk, highland, jazz, modern, and tap to mention just a few. The advantage of going to a spring dance recital is that you and your child can see the various types of dance available in this dance school. Seeing all the different dances can help your child decide which one appeals.

Recreation centers offer dance programs as well. The advantage of a recreation center program is that they usually offer a shorter course - an 8 week session instead of an 8 month session. Talk to other parents who have their children enrolled in dance programs and ask how pleased they are with the instruction their children have received. Like with music, work on your part will be required to find a dance program and teacher to suit your child.

Formal dance lessons don't have to start when your child is 4. Like music lessons, there is often very little progress in dance classes for small children. Ballet in particular is a very demanding form of dance and can move very slowly for small children. Your child may be just as happy dancing around on his own in your home or in the backyard.   Holly's experience with a dance class when she was 4 years old was not quite what she'd hoped. A few years later, she, Robin, Josh and I took folk dance classes together. It was a great deal of fun to be in an adult class. The other adults were thrilled to have dancers under 45 years old. We were happy because we spent the time dancing not waiting for the teachers to do crowd control.

When Holly was ready to try other forms of dance, she started taking private tap and ballet lessons with a homeschooled dancer. In the three years since she started, Holly has caught up to her age peers in ballet. Starting later has not been a handicap.

Dance is a physical act as well as an expressive act. Physical activity is a daily necessity for all human beings. It is absolutely essential for children's well being. The density of their bones when they are older is partly determined by the amount of exercise they have as children. That's why I have included physical education in this chapter. I think that the movement of the human body is an art whether it is in dance, gymnastics, running, swimming, bowling, playing tennis, etc. Encourage your children in physical activity by doing it yourself. Go for walks, go swimming, play outdoor games like frisbee, baseball, kickball, hide and seek, etc.

If your child shows a special interest in a particular form of physical activity look for programs that will give your children skills to improve their abilities. Like looking for a music teacher or a dance program, do some talking with other parents, look around at what is available before signing up.

Keep in mind that you don't have to sign up for a program to get physical exercise. Walking to parks, jogging on trails, going swimming, playing catch, jumping rope, etc. are all things you can do with your children without instruction. One advantage to homeschooling your children is that during school hours parks, tennis courts, swimming pools, and the like are not as crowded because most children are in school. We enjoy this calm and peaceful atmosphere in public places.

Sometimes, my boys would become so involved in their play with Lego blocks, that they would have been inside all day just using their small muscles. I would go out with them after supper and we'd go for a walk or have a game of tag or do something to exercise their big muscles. Mothers need to go out and use their big muscles as well. It's refreshing.

Visual Art

I mentioned the importance of having art materials available in the second chapter - paints, crayons, pencils, modeling material, and paper. When my children were younger, we did most of our art work in the kitchen. It made cleanup simpler. I encouraged my children to draw every day by taking out paper and pencils and drawing things myself. When we painted, I covered the kitchen table with newspaper, and brought out the water color paintboxes and tablets. The children would paint for an hour or so. When they were young, the artwork came from each child's imagination.

A friend gave my boys some art lessons for a few months when they were 10, 8, and 5 years old. She had them draw from life - boots, stuffed birds we borrowed from the museum, still-life arrangements, etc. This was fun for them. She did not tell them to draw any certain way, just encouraged them to look at things and try to draw them. At the time, Noah, who was 8, drew very tiny pictures. Sandra encouraged him to draw on a larger scale. Noah continued to develop his skills and is a very talented artist. He particularly likes to draw people. He has had no other instruction. Instead he looks at other art work, the world around him, and experiments on his own. Being at home has allowed him time to develop his gift.

No matter what skill level your child has, the act of creating with paint or pencil on paper is important and fun. Drawing is not only for those who are talented. It is a way of communicating no matter what the skill level involved. The Chinese proverb "One picture is worth a thousand words" is worth keeping in mind. A child may be able to express himself in drawings and other art work much more readily than in words. Learning to write and read depends on learning codes that may not seem very sensible to a child. That same child may be able to use a paintbrush and communicate with his own personal symbols that reveal more subtle and complex ideas and emotions than the child is capable of expressing in words. Drawing and painting comes directly from the subconscious mind and allows a child an opportunity to develop that part of himself.

Like anything, the more drawing or painting one does the greater the skill one acquires. Encourage your child to express himself in this way by providing time and materials. I enjoyed being with my children when they were young as they drew or painted. Sometimes I'd draw or paint, too. Other times as they worked at the kitchen table, I cleaned the counters or made supper. If you are unsure about art, you may find reading books like *Drawing on the Right Side of the Brain* or *The Natural Way to Draw* helpful. Another book I found helpful for inspiration was *emphasis: ART* by Wachowiak and Ramsay. This is a textbook published by Intext Educational Publishers. I used these books to give me some ideas. However, when I set up the kitchen table for painting or drawing, I gave no instruction on how to draw or paint, unless asked for help, other than how to use the materials like a watercolor paint box and to define the rules regarding the activity (painting - on the paper not the chairs, etc.) when they painted or drew.

When we used a specific technique such as wax resist crayon

drawings and black paint, I gave them an example first to demonstrate how it worked. This technique was always popular to do at Hallowe'en, when we drew scary pictures with crayons and then covered our pictures with black paint. It was magic to watch the paint bead up over the crayoned parts.

Another thing that's easy to use is the foam trays that come under meat or other food items for printing. Draw a picture in the foam with a pencil, then put on ink and print. There are lots of books in the library that have suggestions for art projects and techniques if you want ideas and instructions.

Origami (Japanese paper folding) is something else we have all enjoyed doing. There are many books available that come complete with instructions. See the bibliography for this chapter for titles of books we found easy to use. Paper folding seems to lead to paper cutting and snowflakes and other folded and cut paper projects. *Pleasure with Paper* by Breda is a book I enjoyed that gives instruction for many things including paper dolls holding hands. I find it helpful to look through books like this to give me new ideas.

It is important to provide your child with good quality tools such as scissors that cut well and to show your children how to work safely and respectfully with these tools and other art materials. They will need supervision even after they have learned the skills. Accidents can happen so quickly. Part of teaching your children about how to use tools safely is teaching them how to call the police, fire, and/or emergency department in your vicinity. Even young children need to know how to call an emergency number like 911. I taught my children using dramatic play - we pretended to call 911 and acted out what would happen next.

As children grow older, they may be at home on their own more. It's important to let them know where to reach a parent or a family friend in case of an emergency as well as how to call the fire, police or ambulance service in your community. Basic first-aid is also important for children to know. If you are uncertain about teaching them first-aid consider taking a course together. The Red Cross in the United States and the St. John's Ambulance in Canada offer basic first-aid courses.

Display the art work that your child has created, and not just on the fridge. Talk with him or her about what you see using descriptive words rather than judgmental words. For example - "I see a lot of work went into this picture - there are leaves on all the branches of the trees. You have drawn the grass as individual blades, the blue of the sky is of various shades. I feel peaceful when I look at this picture. If you'd like to tell me what you were thinking of when you drew the picture, I'd like to listen." This gives your child a chance to talk about his or her art work. Your child may or may not talk. For some children this gives an opening to tell mom what they were thinking of. For other children, the act of creating is what was important. Your child may not be able to tell you anything in words. The picture expressed whatever he or she was doing and s/he may find it boring to discuss it. Using descriptive comments instead of value judgments and accepting a child's reticence to talk about his or her picture may require a lot of practice on your part.

Only take a child to art galleries if you have a child who is interested in looking at other people's art work. It can be an opportunity for discussion about what your child did and didn't like. Children tend to move along at various paces in a gallery. Some take a long time at each picture, others zip right through. Keep this in mind when you plan a trip to a gallery.

Picture books are also good sources of art. As my husband and I read stories to our children when they were little, we sometimes stopped reading to point out specific pictures in the books and comment about how the artist had portrayed a certain event or person. (We didn't do this all the time because it can be very disruptive to the story.) We discussed how the pictures made us feel and asked our children how they felt or what they saw. In this way we helped our children develop their visual awareness.

Taking time to notice art work in picture books, on walls in buildings, or just the light shining on a tree branch gives children a background in observing things. It encourages awareness of their surroundings and awareness of their responses to their surroundings.

As well as art to decorate the walls or tables, children can enjoy making things to decorate themselves such as items of clothing. Learning to sew, knit, crochet, or weave can all be fun. As I mentioned in a previous chapter, each of my children knows how to hand sew as well as how to use the sewing machine. At various times, they have made a number of cloth things- finger puppets, costumes, doll clothes, their own clothes. Textile arts are the source of pleasure for a number of adults. Help your children learn some of the basics so that they can discover the pleasure of these ancient crafts. Fabric stores may carry beginning to sew books that have simple projects designed to teach children how to use a sewing machine. There are also sewing courses for children offered in some communities if you don't feel comfortable teaching your child to sew. Again, take time to find out if this course and teacher will be suitable for your child.

Like music, art is a way to express one's emotions and perceptions of the world. Helping your children to express themselves artistically means helping them learn to be keen observers of the world around them and of their own internal world; to pay attention to the feelings created by certain places, sounds, smells, or sights. Encourage your children to be aware of the natural world as the seasons change or as the day turns to night. Being aware in this way, being encouraged to pay attention to these things, will give your child a wealth of experience to draw on for self-expression.

You may feel that your child wants to do things in the field of art that you do not have the ability to help with or the inclination. Look for community programs such as pottery classes, drawing classes, etc. There are also artists who offer individual instruction in most communities. We have many discussions at our house whether or not anyone can teach someone else to be an artist. I think that exposure to art forms may be what is most helpful in taking classes, and the encouragement and support that these classes can provide. Make sure that any class your child takes is supportive and builds on strengths.

Dramatic Arts

Drama is another form of expression that children enjoy. My children have not done drama in any formal way. However, their play has always had a dramatic element. Our dress-up clothes have been used as costumes for foresters in the time of Robin Hood, pirates, knights, and in many other ways. As they played in these dress-up clothes, they enacted many dramas with on going stories for themselves not for an audience. In the next chapter, I will talk more about this dramatic play and how it has been part of our social studies curriculum.

Live theater captures our imaginations and takes us to another world. It is magical. Finding good quality live theater for children is not easy. Explore library story hours as there are often drama groups that put on special events for libraries. Sometimes there are drama or storytelling groups that perform in elementary schools. If you have developed a good relationship with your local public school, you can ask them to let you know about any performances that will be coming to the school.

I'd suggest that before you attend any live performance (even those at your local school) that you do a bit of research about the show. If you were unable to do research or even if you've re-searched the show and find that it is unsuitable, leave! Also for the sake of others in the audience, if your child is not happy and is asking to leave, listen to your child and leave. The performers have worked hard to produce their show and the rest of the audience has come to watch the show not listen to an unhappy child. No program is so good that it is worth having your child frightened or unhappy. If you want to talk with your child, the lobby is the best place, not in the theater where you will disturb the others in the audience.

Some children may be interested in learning more about acting and putting on live theater productions. Like looking for dance or music teachers, do some research and watch some productions put on by any theater classes in your community. In some places, there are enough interested homeschoolers to form a drama club and put on productions.

Movies and TV shows are another source of drama. With these, like with live theater, use your discretion. As Marie Winn writes in *The Plug-In Drug*, TV can take over people's lives. We chose not to have a TV for many years. We acquired one after Noah became diabetic. Two years previously we had started a tradition of renting a TV and a VCR for a month during the time of the World Series. Being able to watch baseball games was important for Noah right after he came home from the hospital.

The TV hasn't changed our lives as much as I once thought it might because we find very little to watch that interests us. Perhaps because all of our children have been read to so frequently, they prefer books to what TV has to offer. A VCR can be a useful tool for families to use to watch movies. One great advantage to using a VCR to see movies is that you can stop the movie, rewind it and see a sequence again, or you can stop and discuss things with each other, and then proceed. Something I do frequently when I read a story aloud but I can't do when we watch a TV show together.

What movies and plays do is tell us a story about people's lives - the choices they make, and how those choices effect them and their relationships with the other people in their lives. The stories in movies and plays have a strong effect because they are visual. They can transport us out of ourselves into another world, place, or time. Stories told aloud can have that effect, too. Listening to a good story told by a good storyteller is a joy. Children respond with attention, quiet and enthrallment to storytelling. It can be a simple retelling of an old and well known fairy tale such as "Cinderella" or "The Three Little Pigs" or it can be a brand new story that engages us. Tell your children stories as well as reading to them. Listen to their stories as they tell them to you.

In Chapter 4, I mentioned writing down children's stories. Encourage them to tell their stories as well and record them on audio-cassettes. Even young children enjoy telling stories. Their stories often include all the integral parts of a story - the play of words, the development of characters and the solving of a problem - especially if they have heard lots of stories. Storytelling encourages the development of the imagination. Sometimes telling stories has been equated with telling lies. I think of a series of children's books about a woman named Mrs. Piggywiggle that I used to read as a child. Mrs. Piggywiggle would "cure" the children in town of their various bad habits including one little boy who "told stories" (lies). That little boy had an incredible gift for storytelling - the adults around him believed whatever he said. When I reread the story as an adult I wanted to change it and have Mrs. Piggywiggle acknowledge his talent - his incredible imagination and gift for telling a believable story - and find a way to help this boy utilize his active imagination and gift more positively rather than making his "bad habit" disappear.

Storytellers need to have a vivid imagination as well as a gift for making their imaginary world come alive for their listeners so that their audience can enter into the story. A storyteller we have enjoyed tremendously is Jay O'Callahan. He makes up the most wonderful tales and transports his listeners into his imaginary worlds. "*Herman and Marguerite* is miraculous. ...This story is practically an epic and it's about worms." - Entertainment Weekly. "Jay O'Callahan is like a prodigious one-man band in his ability to single-handedly create a cast of characters and set rich and complex scenes." - Parents' Choice Award. Look for his recordings in your local library or call him at 1-800-626-5356, Artana, Box 1054, Marshfield, MA. 02050 and ask for a catalogue. You can also go to his web site. See the bibliography for this chapter for his URL. We have enjoyed each of his stories. They became a part of our lives. We use certain key phrases from his stories in our own conversations to illustrate a point - "Give him a pickle to quiet him down." or "It's a good game. It's a good game." He tells stories for older listeners, too, that are autobiographical and very moving. I encourage you to find his recordings. His stories are unique and wonderful.

To conclude this chapter, I'd like to re-emphasize how important the arts are for your child. I think we were born to create - be it a poem, a garden, a song, a pleasant space, a drawing, a cake, a dance, etc. The form isn't as important as the doing, the creating. Homeschooling allows children time to pursue creative activities. My children's creative activities have been the source of their education. In the process of play - be it dramatic, physical (like sports), musical, or artistic - they have learned about the world, people, animals, plants, etc. Encourage and support your children by providing materials, space, your attention, new points of view, live performances by both amateurs and professionals, discussions, teachers (when needed), descriptive comments about their creations, and your sincere appreciation of their efforts.

Robin as a knight 1988

CHAPTER 7
Life as Curriculum:
Science and Social Studies

When I was in high school in a suburb of Chicago from 1962-1966, I assumed that what I was being required to learn to graduate and become an "educated" person was the standard and complete body of knowledge for all high schools across the U.S.A., that anyone with a high school diploma would know the same things that I knew. I've found out since then that my assumption was incorrect.

I've asked my friends (who were in high school during the 60's, 70's, and 80's in both the United States and Canada) and my husband (who was in high school in the 60's in Louisville, Ky.) about their high school educations. What they learned did not coincide with what I had learned. I expected that there would be some difference, but the differences were much greater than I expected. These differences tell me that what I had been led to believe as being absolutely essential to know wasn't necessarily so. These differences helped me to see that an educated person is defined by cultural values of time and place.

As I described the way in which I helped my children with reading, writing and math in the previous chapters, you probably noticed that I did not follow a set curriculum or use textbooks. Our curriculum has been based on whatever interests my children have. Using these interests, I helped them gain a mastery of what I consider to be the skills necessary for living in the world today. These include being able to read fluently and with pleasure, write fluently, understand arithmetic well enough to balance a checkbook, learn how to manage money, understand basic nutrition to maintain health, learn how to pursue an idea or project, and learn to think critically and imaginatively. Because the body of material an educated person is expected to learn and know shifts with time and cultural bias, my goal has been to help my children become competent in the skills listed above so that they can use these skills to acquire any information or knowledge that they may need as they grow older.

In the book *If You Want to Be Rich and Happy, Don't Go to School*, the author, Robert T. Kiyosaki, discusses the importance of being a generalist. He emphasizes how disabling it can be to be trained in only one subject and not understand how to go about acquiring new training or information that one might need say particularly after a job loss. Learning how to acquire information has been the main focus of our homeschooling.

Before going any further, let me go to my dictionary again. *The New Lexicon Webster's Encyclopedic Dictionary of The English Language Canadian Edition* defines curriculum as " a course of study, esp. at school or college; a list of the courses offered at a school, college, or university [Latin = a running race]"

Just as we did not use textbooks for reading, writing, or math, we did not for science, history, or geography. Instead, we have followed our interests as our curriculum or course of study. It is only in the world of academics that separate fields of study exist. Separate fields of study are a convenience to make the amazing chaos and beauty of life on our planet somewhat more understandable from our human point of view. However, fields of study, like dissection, divide up the whole, and often the whole is more than the sum of its parts. It can be a useful way to learn about the whole, yet it is important to keep in mind that this separation is a created convenience and only describes a portion of the whole.

With this in mind let's explore some of the ways you can use your every day experiences to the fullest and enable your children to have a richer appreciation and understanding of the wonderful complexity of life. Let's take making a salad for example. Let me show you how making a salad can be a course of study that covers biology, sociology, physiology, geography, chemistry, language arts, and meteorology.

We've had some interesting discussions about lettuce as we made salads (language arts), i.e., where and how it is grown (geography, chemistry, biology, agricultural practices). In the summer, we pick it out of the garden which leads to discussions about bugs and slugs. Because we garden organically and do not use pesticides, we tend to have slugs in our lettuce. One day at supper, we were discussing slugs and I had an opportunity to relate the way I used to trap slugs when I lived in Cape Breton, Nova Scotia as a self-sufficient farmer. We discussed the difference in climate between Victoria, where we live, and Cape Breton (meteorology). I told them I used to use beer in little plastic dishes to attract the slugs. The slugs would crawl in attracted by the beer, and then drown in the beer (biology). This then led to a discussion of alcoholic beverages and why people drink them (sociology).

Baseball was often a major topic of discussion in our house. The boys used to keep track of the batting averages of many players (statistics). They read about baseball players in the newspaper and kept track of the salaries earned (economics), the drugs some players use (sociology, human physiology), the trades that are made (statistics and strategic thinking). Each of them knows where the cities are that have major league baseball teams (geography). They have a great store of information about which team won which pennant when (history). They are aware of the differences between knuckleballs and fast balls (physics) and the consequences of certain injuries for a player's future ability to play (human physiology, economics). We have had discussions about the high salaries players receive at such young ages (psychology, economics); the process of resolving the baseball strike of 1994 (sociology, psychology, history). When they were 17 and 15 years old, Josh, Noah and I watched a film, *Bingo Long and The Travelling All Stars*, about an African American baseball team and the beginning of integration in sports and discussed it (African American studies, history, race relations).

I am sure if you think about it you can find similar opportunities in your family's life for discussion and exploration that will broaden everyone's understanding. Homeschooling your child allows you to have many opportunities to engage your children in this sort of discussion. When a child is particularly intrigued by an aspect of life, say horses, you can use that subject as your curriculum. You can go to see actual horses, perhaps give your child an opportunity to ride. You can learn with your child all about the history of horses and the various breeds. This can be done both through nonfiction and fiction books.

Sometimes, fictional accounts of people and their relationships with horses are more meaningful than just reading a list of facts about horses. Books like *Misty of Chincoteague* by Margeruite Henry give a child a glimpse of what it's like to have a pony and train her. If you go to the library, you can find many other books about the subject of horses. If a child can not easily read on her own, you can read them aloud. Don't wait until a child has mastered the basic skills of reading to pursue the things that interest that child.

Because I have four children, I have had the opportunity to learn about a lot of things that I would not necessarily have chosen to learn on my own as I helped them pursue their own interests. At the same time, they shared my interests such as gardening when they were younger.

Science

Because of the experiences I have had, the books I have read, and the choices I have made, much of the information my children have learned from me in the field of science has been related to gardening, animals, and health. We dug in the dirt and observed the bugs, the consistency of the soil, the size of the rocks, and the smell of the soil. We spent time observing how the seeds grew into plants, which birds came to the garden, and how fast things grew. This was done as we worked in the garden, as we prepared a meal, or as we went on walks.

When my two older boys were 7 and 5 years old they were fascinated by magnets, electricity, how fast things went, and magic tricks. We visited electronics shops and stocked up on the basics: wires, batteries and battery holders, little light bulbs and holders, and small electric motors so that they could learn about how circuits worked. They did lots of experiments on their own, figuring out how to follow diagrams and how to design their own circuits.

They also enjoyed experiments with vinegar and baking soda. Although this could have been an opportunity for me to explain chemical formulas and how a base and an acid interact to produce gas, I didn't. I had a 2 year old to look after, and could only do so much. Josh and Noah were happy with the basic explanation I gave them and just enjoyed observing the effect. If they had been really keen on understanding this more thoroughly, I am sure they would have continued to ask questions because they did at other times when they wanted more information.

I want to stress how easy it can be to use a child's interest as your curriculum. A child who is fascinated by dinosaurs can learn a lot about many fields of study as well as learn about reading, writing and math. Pacing out just how big a Tyrannosaurus Rex was, is a fun way to do math. Drawing pictures of what the world may have looked like when there were dinosaurs can help children be aware of the food cycle, etc. In other words, if you start anywhere, you will find many layers and side paths to explore that will lead you and your child in all sorts of interesting directions.

At the same time as you encourage your children's interests, you don't have to use every question or interest as a "teachable moment." In fact, it's impossible to do this. It would drive everyone crazy. My children made it fairly obvious when they wanted to know more and when they'd had enough. "Stop, Mom, we just want to play."

You may feel that you are not knowledgeable enough to help your child pursue various interests in the field of science. As I mentioned in previous chapters, you don't have to teach you children everything yourself when you homeschool. If your child has an interest that you know very little about, and have no interest in learning anymore about, look for someone who does have the knowledge and ask this person to work with your child. Instructors are often quite surprised by the self-motivation of homeschooled children.

You can participate by helping your child learn to evaluate the experience. One way to do this is to describe to your child what you see as the child gets ready for this activity or while the child is engaged in the activity. "When you get ready to go riding, you're always ready 15 minutes early, eagerly waiting. You must really like riding." or "You seem to go inside yourself when it is time to go riding. You're not smiling. How are you feeling about riding?" Learning to evaluate an activity to see if it is still suitable is a skill that I want my children to learn. To be able to assess the pros and cons of a situation and determine if it is of value is useful for a child and even more useful for an adult. I mentioned something about this in the last chapter in regard to practicing a musical instrument. Learning about one's likes and dislikes, one's goals, and one's hopes helps a child begin to set priorities. With experience in evaluating activities, children gain an understanding of themselves, useful when making career choices.

Moving back to the subject of curriculum - with the understanding that anything can be used as your curriculum - following your child's interests gives you a core curriculum or course of studies. If the passion for information about dinosaurs changes, you can use the next interest in the same way. Your child hasn't lost anything by changing interest, instead, he gained an understanding of the world of dinosaurs. Both of you will gain further knowledge as other interests are pursued.

As an example of living everyday science, our pets have been a great way to learn about zoology. We have had gerbils, parakeets, cats, guinea pigs, rabbits, chickens, and a goldfish. At the present time, we have five cats, two mothers and three of their daughters, as well as two guinea pigs and a dwarf rabbit. We find it fascinating to watch the interaction of our cats and their different personalities. When the two older cats had kittens, we enjoyed watching the kittens grow. One of our cats, Charlotte, had her kittens in Josh's bed. Holly was only three at the time, but she can still remember watching one of them be born.

Taking care of the various pets meant learning about these animals - their natural habitat; their reproduction cycle; their natural predators; their natural diet; their ways of dealing with shock, trauma, or injury; and their responses to human interaction. Holly has expressed a desire for a puppy at various times in her life. Because of the care she has given some of our other animals, she is able to be realistic about what would be required to take care of a puppy. She has decided that she doesn't really want to take care of a puppy every day. Instead, she goes to see some of our friends who have dogs and no children. She has a great time with their dogs, and then comes home. Holly realizes that part of owning a dog is taking care of it's bowel movements, and she hasn't been prepared to do that.

Robin with Elf 1987

Holly with Cuddles 1989

If at all possible, include some sort of pet in your family life. Guinea pigs are fairly easy to take care of and can easily be kept in a cage indoors. Their living quarters need to be cleaned regularly, so a child will need help to clean and change the bedding. Check with a pet store or breeder for the right kind of housing or check the library for books about guinea pigs or other animals. Take time to do the research required to find out just what is involved in having a particular kind of pet.

If you acquire a pet, you will need to help your child learn how to handle the pet gently. You will need to be willing to help your child learn how to take care of the pet. Children under 7-years-old cannot be expected to regularly feed and take care of pets. They will need assistance. It is unfair for an animal to suffer because a child is not able to be a responsible caretaker at all times. You'll also have to take care of injuries that may happen. As your child grows older, he or she will be more able to take over all of the care and feeding of a pet.

Taking care of a live animal can be a delight for a child. Pets can bring children tremendous joy. There is something wonderfully soothing about stroking an animal. An animal can give a child a gift of love and affection, and a child can give love, affection, and care to an animal. This gives a child a sense of being important, mattering to another living being who is not human.

Something else to consider when thinking about getting a pet is that pets die. It is important to help your child deal with the grief experienced when a pet dies. There are many books about death and dying (these are written about people but can be useful in the death of a pet) that may help you at a time like this. Death brings up many questions about life and it's purpose. What you do to help your child if a pet dies, helps both of you to come to a better understanding of your particular belief system. If a child is supported as he grieves, than the hurt of the loss passes and healing takes place. Some people offer the well meaning advice, that as soon as a pet dies, replace the pet with another one. I think it is important for a child to have time to feel the loss. The loss is there and real whether or not we are willing to recognize it. Unlike a broken toy, pets are not interchangeable. Take time after the death of a pet to allow your child to grieve.

So what happens if your child expresses no particular interests? Then you might need to try reading lots of different stories about lots of different people and situations. You might need to listen to lots of different kinds of music. You might need to explore your natural environment together and talk together to see if there isn't something that intrigues your child.

At certain times, it seems as though there is nothing that interests a child. A child who was busy and content suddenly becomes bored and grumpy. I think these stages in a child's life are related to physical growth spurts, particularly ages 10-12. Everything may seem boring to your child. This is a difficult time both for you and your child and it is a normal state of development. It is almost as though a child is discarding everything that used to be fun or exciting in order to make room for new ideas and interests, yet those new interests are not always as quick to appear as the boredom with the old. I wish I had a quick fix answer. This is a time when you must work hard as a mother to maintain a relationship with your child free from blaming him/her for this state as well as free of accepting the blame for your child's boredom (as long as you have done your part by providing a stimulating learning environment for your child - see Chapter 2). Your child needs to know you are available and supportive but that at a certain point in his life you are unable to make his dissatisfaction go away.

This dissatisfaction is a natural phenomenon - like rain and sunshine. It is also like the stage of labor in childbirth called transition. During this transition stage of labor, I felt, as many women have, that I would rather not have a baby after all. I felt like saying "Let's just forget the whole thing." Intellectually, I knew about this stage which helped me because I was aware that it would happen, but it did not change the fact that I needed to go through the stage and experience it. Between contractions, I would remember that I had done this before and the pushing part would come soon, leading to a baby being born. I could hardly wait to get to the pushing part. However during a contraction I would forget and I wanted to stop and not have a baby after all. Perhaps, if you could think of yourself as a labor coach for your child as he or she goes through the transitions of physical growth spurts, it might make it easier for both of you.

One of the most important things to remember as a homeschooling mother is that your children will not be happy, busy, self-motivated learners all the time. That's impossible. It's normal and expected that children will be unhappy or lonely or bored. When they are young and express their boredom in unacceptable physical ways, it might be a good time to go for a walk, a run, a swim, or a change of locality - such as going outside. As they grow older, you can share with them what you do when you are bored, how you cope when you feel as they do.

As I said before, there is no easy, quick-fix solution to this situation. What is required is time and patience. Keep reading stories, keep talking to your child, offer to help explore other possibilities, and accept that there will be difficult times. However, as stated in Chapter 2, a child needs to understand that the expression of his or her unhappiness needs to be respectful of others.

I hope that the examples I have used to illustrate "Life as Curriculum" are helpful. Keep in mind that not all homeschoolers are as unstructured about curriculum as I am. Many use textbooks to guide their studies. *Homeschooling For Excellence* by David and Micki Colfax describes a more textbook oriented approach to learning at home. You may find it helpful if you are looking for more information about which textbooks to use. You can also find advertising about various curriculum materials in such magazines as *Home Education Magazine* (www.home-ed-magazine.com) or search the internet for information about homeschooling.

No matter how homeschooling takes place, one of the benefits of homeschooling is that a child has control over time in a different way than a child in school. If a certain topic is of great interest, than the child can pursue it without being told that "The period is over. Time to start another subject." One of the other benefits is the companionship of their parents and siblings.

Here is a list of some books with a scientific slant that I have found helpful as we explored the world around us. The books that follow are ones that I have enjoyed using with my children, ones that they have enjoyed on their own, or books that I found helpful so that I became more knowledgeable about a certain topic.

Bet You Can and *Bet You Can't* by Vicki Cobb. Both of these books have fun science tricks that our children enjoyed doing. Vicki Cobb has written a number of books about the science of everyday objects that you may find interesting.

The Magic School Bus books by Joanna Cole illustrated by Bruce Degen. The stories take place in a classroom as the children study different science topics with Miss Frizzle their teacher. My favorite is *The Magic School Bus at The Waterworks.* The children become as small as raindrops and participate in the whole cycle of how water is carried to people's homes and then used and recycled. (There's a Tom Chapin song "The Wheel of the Water" on his recording *Mother Earth* that describes this process in song.) This book and the others in the series impart information with humor. We enjoyed these as picture books when my children were quite young. As they grew older, they still enjoyed the books, retaining more information because of their age and greater experience.

Eyewitness Juniors - a whole series of books on Amazing Mammals, Birds, Snakes, Spiders, etc. Good illustrations, both drawings and photographs and lots of facts in small paragraphs in various places on the page. Good for children 4-5 years old as well as older ones who can read on their own and enjoy learning about animals. Available in paperback, published by Alfred A. Knopf.

Harper and Row publishes a whole series of I-Can-Read Science books that most libraries carry in their primary reading section. One of our favorites was *Benny's Animals* by Millicent Selsam.

Show your children where the nonfiction books are kept in the library and how to find those subjects that especially interest them. Help them to feel comfortable browsing through both the fiction and nonfiction sections of the library.

The main thing to keep in mind as you homeschool your child is that your own curiosity sets a model for your child. If you enjoy learning new things or exploring new ideas, your child more than likely will, too. You need to be honest and only show an interest if you actually have an interest in a subject. I bought electrical equipment to make it possible for my boys to explore how circuits worked, but I didn't participate in their experiments beyond the basics. They explored on their own. Talking about our cats or about plants was different. Animal and gardening topics are easy for me to be enthusiastic about because they interest me.

What is important when homeschooling is to be able to support your child genuinely in his own interests. If that interest is not one you can share, find someone else who can. Teachers' associations may have a list of unemployed teachers who are available for tutoring. It can be a very rewarding relationship for both child and tutor if you can find someone who's enthusiasm is genuine and with whom your child enjoys working. By finding others who can help your child pursue an interest, you show your child that you respect and support the child's need for knowledge and information beyond your expertise.

Think of Gerald Durrell (whom I mentioned in Chapter 2) as an example. His family was not knowledgeable about natural history, but they either supported or tolerated his interest. Each of the members of his family had certain passions in life. It was accepted and expected. As an adult, he continued his passion for animals and became a collector of rare and almost extinct animals. He established breeding programs for them in his own zoo, The Jersey Preservation Trust. One of the ways he raised funds for his zoo was through his writing about his life as a child in Corfu and his life as a collector of animals. His books are great read alouds, filled with humor and lots of natural history information about insects, animals, and people.

I hope this very brief look at science study gives you some ideas. From my point of view, observation and sharing one's observations are the foundations of science study. Children learning at home have many opportunities to observe the world around them as well as many opportunities to manipulate objects and observe the effects of those manipulations. Like with mathematics, science is often defined by vocabulary. Science is a part of life and doesn't have to be studied divorced from life.

Some children may show a particular interest in a branch of science that may need special nurturing by you or someone else. One of the benefits of homeschooling is that a child with a particular interest can have time to pursue it. To close this section on science let me quote from the forward of *Absolute Zero Gravity: A collection of jokes, anecdotes, and riddles, revealing the funny side of physics, biology, mathematics and other branches of science* by Betsy Devine and Joel E. Cohen: "Scientists are funny people. Not just the great ones who think they have discovered the secret of life or of the brain or of the common cold. Even ordinary day-to-day scientists are funny, because they all think that the world makes sense! Most people know better."

Josh harvesting pumpkins 1987

Social Studies

As with science, I used opportunities as they arose to bring history and geography into our lives. Family history was our starting place as my children liked hearing stories about when I was younger or stories about their father's and grandparents' lives. I used stories almost exclusively to present historical information. There is something so appealing in stories. As Robert Coles, author of *The Call of Stories* (and many other books) says "It is the perspective, the morality, the way in which people view the information of their lives that give things meaning." (He taught literature courses at Yale Medical and Law School to introduce future doctors and lawyers to some of the ethical questions of their professions through situations presented in literature.) This book affirmed my own feeling that I have learned more from novels about people and how they have been affected by the circumstances of their lives than from any history book.

Before we had the printed word, we had stories. Stories were the way people remembered where they came from, who they were as a people, how to live their lives, and when it was time to do the things that needed to be done. Stories have given people pleasure, taught valuable lessons, and given spiritual succor for ages.

Bedtime story reading has been a 365 day a year event in our house since Josh was 1½ years old. During the years of bedtime and other reading, I read many stories about people's lives in other times and other places. As my children grew older, we covered a lot of historical ground by reading books by authors who have written historical fiction for children: Ian Serralier, Kate Seredy, Rosemary Sutcliffe, Geoffrey Trease are just a few of the ones we have enjoyed. The stories I read my children brought us in touch with many cultures, many historical periods, and many people's lives. As we read, we took time to discuss the characters, their actions, decisions, and thoughts. These characters became our friends, a part of our lives. (In retrospect, I realize that I did more of the work of homeschooling at bedtime - reading stories, discussing stories, or discussing other matters my children brought up - than at any other time of the day.)

Let me give you an example. I read a series of three books to Holly by Beatrice Hunter about a girl named Margaret who goes to live with her aunt and uncle (*A Place for Margaret, Margaret In The Middle, Margaret On Her Way*). The series takes place in Ontario, Canada during the 1930s. It presents a detailed picture of life in a large family during the Depression years. I then read *Cheaper by The Dozen* and *Belles on Their Toes* to both Holly and Robin, also about a large family during the same time period but in the United States. As a result of these stories, Holly and I had some very interesting discussions about families and how mothers and children relate to each other.

Holly very astutely observed that if a mother wasn't breastfeeding her baby anybody could take care of that baby. She also wondered when women stopped nursing their babies and why. (Good questions!) We discussed the Industrial Revolution and how that affected mothers and babies. We talked about the change from an agriculture economy to an industrial economy. It was fun and exciting. I was pleased and surprised by Holly's perception that artificial infant feeding has a great impact on a mother and child's relationship.

I loved these types of discussions that I've had with my children. These discussions were a forum for critical thinking. They provided an opportunity for my children to express their thoughts. They provided a place for them to share their perceptions. Discussing the characters in a story gave us a chance to talk about values, goals, and moral choices. It gave us a chance to talk about how people in different times and places made decisions.

Stories give perspective and help us to see the world through another person's point of view. Stories can help put facts in a framework. *The Little House Books* by Laura Ingalls Wilder are a good example: she makes the facts of pioneers moving West real. I've read this series of books aloud three times to various groupings of my children. As I read them aloud, I took time to share my reactions to some of the things "Ma" said. We discussed how differently "Pa" and "Ma" related to their children, etc. We enjoyed the glimpse into the events of Laura's childhood. We were also aware of how differently people thought at that time, i.e., Ma saying she "Didn't like to go to the store for every little thing."

Some of those ways of thinking irritated me - "Ma's" dislike of Indians, the total subservience of women to men. Some of the incidents that described the behavior expected of men and women at the time helped me to gain a better understanding of some of our present day difficulties. I discussed my reactions and thoughts with my children. They enjoyed telling me what they thought about what a character said or did.

I also try to connect an incident in a story that I am reading aloud to our own personal family history - "Grandma was born about the same time as so and so in this story." This helps us to have a new understanding of Grandma. Roger Lee McBride has done a series of books about Laura's daughter Rose that continues the story of Laura and her family. They are delightful. There are now books available about Caroline, Laura's mother, written by Maria D. Wilkes; stories about Charlotte who is Caroline's mother and Laura's grandmother by Melissa Wiley; and Martha who is Charlotte's mother, Caroline's grandmother, and Laura's great-grandmother by Melissa Wiley. These are all published by Harper Trophy. It's fun to have this collection of stories of these 5 generations of women.

Another series of books that we have enjoyed about a family is about a girl named Anastasia Krupnik (and that's the title of the first book in the series) by Lois Lowry. These are not historical - but they do describe life in the 1970's and 80's. They are great read alouds and quite funny. I have read them aloud twice and wouldn't mind reading them aloud a few more times. Lois Lowry captures the character of Anastasia so well starting when Anastatia is 10 and up through her 13th year.

The discussions that we have had as a result of a story that I have read are as important as the story. We discuss how these characters make decisions. This gives us an opportunity to explore how we make decisions, and a chance to look at our values. I think this type of discussion is vital. It gives children a chance to practice discretion, discernment, and judgment. We are bombarded with information and choices everyday. How do we decide which piece of information to use when we make decisions? How do we judge the accuracy or the application of a certain fact to our situation?

We need the wisdom that stories contain. We often have more than enough information. What we need help with is how to sort that information so that it can be useful in our lives. We need the works of fiction, fairy tales, and myth because they address the age old questions of mankind. The outer circumstances have changed and more often than not we do not have something as easily visible as a dragon to fight, but the inner struggles of our lives remain the same.

My children have heard enough fairy tales to know the structure of a fairy tale. They are aware of the various twists and turns that happen in such a tale. For example, the old woman whose nose is stuck in a tree on the path to your destination may be more important than the destination. Fairy tales and myths reach beyond our intellectual understanding to a deeper place within us. Like art and music, they reach into our souls.

Stories can serve to guide us in our own times of trouble. We can turn to stories of people or children in difficult circumstances and draw strength from their survival. Stories about how children coped during the Second World War were important for Noah when he was about 9 years old. *The Silver Sword, The Chestry Oak, The House of Sixty Fathers*, and *Number the Stars* were inspiring for him because they were filled with children's courage. These stories and others like them help us to see our own suffering and worries, our lives, in a larger context. And isn't that the point of history?

Taking a detour from the topic of history, I want to mention that while I have used my children's interests as a starting point for some of our reading, exploring, etc., I have not blindly followed their interests. I think about the 8 year old girl who was killed in an airplane crash in 1996 while flying the plane with her instructor and father present. They were trying to establish a record of some sort and took off in inclement weather. The girl's mother was quoted in my local paper as stating that flying was something her daughter loved to do and she wouldn't keep her from it. I want to be clear that in helping your child follow his or her interests, you need to use your discretion.

I spoke about safety in Chapter 2 - creating a safe space both physically and emotionally. If a child is not allowed to drive a car before reaching the age of 16, why was a child flying an airplane at age 8? Children of that age have barely developed the cones and rods in their eyes necessary to see peripherally to cross the street, how could a child of that age be able to sort out all the factors needed to fly an airplane?

This is an important issue. As a parent it is your responsibility to protect your children from harm. We need to work carefully to create a safe path for our children to walk as they pursue their interests. We want them to reach adulthood! Encouraging your child to pursue his interests doesn't mean that you must do whatever the child wants. It means using a child's interests as a way to learn about the world. It means finding and then doing age appropriate or developmentally appropriate activities in the field of interest. I can't emphasize enough how important it is to use your discretion - to develop your powers of discernment so that you can guide your children as they learn.

I hope that this chapter has given you some ideas to use to explore the different interests and ideas your children have. Science and social studies are a window, a point of view on life. They do not define life. When homeschooling, the opportunity for an interdisciplinarian way of learning is limited only by your resources.

A good example of an inter-disciplinarian way of looking at life is the TV series, *The Day the Universe Changed.* James Burke takes a number of turning points in history such as the development of movable type and shows some of the events that led up to that particular turning point and the repercussions this event has had on the present. (There is an accompanying book that I find helps me to remember what he has said.) He combines science, history, art, music, philosophy, etc. to explore these events. A great example of life as curriculum. The series is adult oriented. I wouldn't recommend it for children under 13, mainly because I don't think younger children would find it very interesting. He does a lot of talking. Of course, you are the best judge of your children's interest and ability to understand and may find that you have a child who is quite intrigued with the program. My two oldest boys found it a fascinating series to watch. It fit right into the way they have studied science and social studies - in context with other events.

I think that we are in the midst of a turning point in regard to education. At one time education was a scarce commodity, a privilege for those who had wealth, tied to a certain locality. With the development of electronic communication, personal computers, and the internet, information is no longer scarce nor is it as privileged. The effects of this will be hard for us to see for many years. (Just as it was hard for those alive during the time of the printing of the *Guttenberg Bible* to predict what effect movable type would have on their society.) Knowledge and/or education is no longer limited to a particular location. It is accessible to almost anyone anywhere. Homeschooling is a part of this change.

I have listed some books and authors that I found helpful within the text of this chapter. There is also a list of authors in the bibliography for this chapter, including the ones I mentioned. Again, use your library and librarians as a resource to fill out the flesh of a topic by providing titles for related fiction and non fiction books. Remember that if you use life as your curriculum, you have the whole world available as subject matter as you homeschool your children. Have fun!

Josh and Noah making apple cider 1990

CHAPTER 8
Burn-out

The stress of mothering is enormous in our North American culture. Add to that the challenge of homeschooling and the potential for burn-out is great. This chapter is devoted to ideas and thoughts about recognizing the signs of burn-out and some suggestions about what to do when feeling overwhelmed and burned-out.

It seems to me that the main source of burn-out and stress is conflict. Although conflict is a normal part of life that can be a great force for action and change, when we are faced with conflict very few of us are comfortable with it. When that conflict is internal conflict, our discomfort increases and our ability to function decreases. Inner conflict can help us to rethink our present attitudes, decisions, or actions. Yet, if we are subject to constant inner conflict, we are overloaded and our circuits burn-out.

Learning how to resolve conflict is vital to successful homeschooling. For me resolving conflict has meant looking at my conflict in the light of my philosophy of education (of life). This takes a lot of work. However, once I've done the work and resolved a particular conflict, life seems to flow more smoothly until another conflict comes along.

Mothering in and of itself can be rife with inner conflict; "Should I be cleaning the house right now, I have a few minutes while everyone is busy? Should I go and find Suzie and read her a story like I said I would? Should I take a few minutes and just sit down and have a cup of tea?" Experienced mothers talk about how often they think perhaps they ought to be doing something other than what they are doing. For new mothers, this constant confusion of what should be done can be as draining as the change in sleep patterns that a new baby brings. Add homeschooling to the load and you add an infinite number of should do's to the many most mothers already have. As a homeschooling mother, you can drive yourself so hard that eventually you come crashing down.

I've found that one of the most important things for me to do to prevent that crash is to limit my sources of both external and internal conflict. When I find myself caught up in conflict, it helps me to look at the problem in terms of needs. Here's an example. When Noah was struggling to learn to read at age 9, much of my panic and inner conflict had to do with other people's expectations. They'd tell me that a child should learn to read by at least 8-years-old or "He's just being lazy and won't read because you read everything to him. You should make him read it himself." I'd question myself and begin to doubt my philosophy of education and my perceptions of the situation. I'd wonder if I was doing Noah a disservice by not pushing him. Then I would look at him and see that I was already pushing him beyond his limits.

My need to have Noah read at age 9 was in conflict with my need to be a competent, capable and supportive teacher - able to work with a child's strengths and build on them. As Noah struggled to learn to read, he began to feel incompetent. Once I was able to see that Noah was doing his best and that I was doing my best and still he wasn't ready to read, I could switch my problem around. I no longer needed to equate Noah's learning to read to my being a competent teacher. I decided to back off and give him time to develop the ability to learn to read. I still worried from time to time, but I would remind myself of why I had made the decision and wait.

When Holly turned 9, she, like Noah, was not ready or able to read the way her brothers Josh and Robin did when they were 9 years old. Holly and I worked together on reading at various times as I wrote about in Chapter 3, but I was not anxious the way I was with Noah. I knew that eventually Holly would learn to read fluently and with pleasure (which she has). I could accept her pace. I was not caught up in the same inner conflict as I had been with Noah. As I mentioned in Chapter 3, Noah began to read fluently at age 12, for Holly it came a little sooner.

I have used this particular example to illustrate how important it is for you to take a close look at what is causing you conflict. Take time to explore your expectations for your child as well as your expectations of yourself. Often, we have a number of hidden expectations, hidden agendas that can cause tremendous turmoil especially if they stay hidden.

I like using the image of the various stages of labor during childbirth to remind myself about how to deal with inner conflict. We all have expectations of how our labor will go. We have dreams of our new baby. However, sometime during the labor we are confronted by the reality of this particular birth and this particular baby. When we can let go of our intellectual control and go with the wisdom of our bodies in the process of labor, birth happens more easily.

Working with our children when helping them learn is similar to this. Quite often we are called on to reevaluate our belief system and take a close look at our child and see how we can best meet this child's needs. We are also called on to have the courage to face our fears about our ability to help our children learn as well as our children's abilities. If we can do all of this with gentleness and patience, often a shift takes place and resolution is born. It is often not quite what we expected. There is no answer already defined waiting for us. We have to develop and find our own answers. This takes time and can be very draining while at the same time it can be tremendously energizing to make these kinds of changes. The book *Expecting Adam* by Martha Beck is a perfect example of the kind of change I mean. Martha Beck wrote this book about her experiences when she was pregnant with her son, Adam, who has Down's syndrome.

As we sort and sift through our thoughts, our children's needs and abilities, our concerns, we can be in constant turmoil, wondering which decision to make and hoping that it is not the wrong one. Perhaps it might help you to know that everyone who homeschools makes mistakes. (Actually, all parents make mistakes. It's what we do with the mistakes when we recognize them that's the important thing.) Most homeschooling mothers question the wisdom of many of their decisions. We are trying something new and have old models for how to do this. One of the problems for many of us in trying this new way of educating our children is that when we went to school we learned that making mistakes was not acceptable. We feel uncomfortable when we make mistakes. We expect perfection of ourselves. We want to score 100% in terms of doing the right things with our children.

Unlike taking a test, homeschooling a child does not come with such clearly defined right answers. You are the one who determines what those right answers are. As in any new situation, we are like nestling birds on their first flight, we will fall for a while before we learn how to use our wings and start our upward ascent. I hope reading about my experiences in this book will help you to find your wings a little sooner.

If you find yourself in constant conflict, accept the conflict and take time to sort out what the issues are. As I mentioned in Chapter 1, the book *People Skills* by Robert Bolton has a section about conflict and problem solving that I have found helpful. Although he does not use examples of inner conflict, instead they are interpersonal, I have found that the techniques can be applied to inner conflict as well as external conflict.

Interpersonal conflict can also be a tremendous drain and cause burn-out. You may find that you and your spouse and/or partner do not see eye to eye about how to go about homeschooling. It is important to take time to work on this and find some way that you can agree to disagree at the very least. You may need to consult with someone who can facilitate communication between you to help you and your partner work things out. Be aware that some people who do this kind of couples' work may have strong feelings about homeschooling and may have a vested interest in the outcome. They may not be able to be neutral about the issue of homeschooling.

You may find that you and your child are in constant conflict. Teaching is an art. It requires a gentle touch and a great deal of willingness on the part of the teacher to figure out how to help a particular person learn. As the adult in the relationship, it is up to you to find a way to solve the conflict.

The conflict that you may be experiencing with your child could be the difficulty of being both teacher and mother. A teacher in school can assign a child to write an essay or do so many pages of math and check the next day to see that it is done. As a homeschooling mother, you do not have the distance that a teacher has. You will be there as your child does this work. If your child is not willing to do this work, you need to use a lot of your energy and patience to help your child complete the work you have assigned. You play two roles, the supportive mother and the demanding teacher. Your child may be angry at you for being a task master, and this may be difficult for both of you.

Some homeschooling families solve this by using correspondence courses. Assignments come from a teacher so the mother and teacher roles are kept separate.

Using the "Life as Curriculum" approach as I have done, there is no separation between the teacher and mother role. The work that I ask my child to do will have an impact on my relationship with that child. I therefore weigh the necessity of that work against the necessity of maintaining a positive relationship with my child. I have described in the other chapters of this book some of the ways I worked with my children to help them learn the basics of reading, writing, and arithmetic while maintaining a positive relationship with them.

Once each child mastered the ability to read, write and do math, my "teaching" as such was over. I no longer asked them to work on any specific learning tasks. Instead, I helped them to pursue their interests.

Take as an example Josh's production of his CDs in October of '96 and Nov. of '97. As well as playing the music, Josh had to make decisions about how to record, where to record, what to record, how to arrange the music recorded, write program notes, design the cover, and how to market his CDs *Josh Layne - A Harp Recital* and *An Afternoon of Harp Music*.   Josh and Noah worked together on these CDs as they did for Josh's first recording *The Eclectic Harp*. Noah painted a picture of Josh's hands for one CD cover and a portrait of Josh playing the harp for the other as well as being the recording engineer.

My role in the process was supportive. I was a coach, a sounding board, a taxi-service, a facilitator, and a finder of equipment. I also became a promoter and marketer.

Going back to interpersonal conflict between a mother and child. Some children take suggestions more readily than others. Some children welcome constant help, others want to be left alone to work things out for themselves. It will take time and patience on your part to find the best way to work with your child. You have already learned a lot about your child as he or she moved through his/her baby and toddler years. You can build on what you have already learned and use this knowledge to best help your child.

I found it such a change to help Robin learn to read after working with Josh and Noah. Robin was not upset if I corrected him. Of course, having worked with his older brothers I asked him if it was OK with him if I corrected him before we started. That probably would have made it easier right from the start with Josh. Robin and I could work together without as much effort on my part. Part of that was who Robin was as well as who I had become after the experience of working with his brothers. Holly, too, has benefited from my greater experience.

Your attitude toward homeschooling is another vital component to assess when you find yourself overwhelmed and burned out. It's important that you do the things you do as a homeschooling mother because you have chosen them based on your values, your commitment, and your philosophy of homeschooling. If you feel that you must do things for other people's reasons, you will not be able to survive.

I think of a conversation my friend, Beth, shared with me. She is a homeschooling mother of three young adults. Beth receives many phone calls from women with questions about homeschooling. She told me about a phone call she had with a woman whose son was interested in learning electronics. "So," she said to Beth, "I guess I have to learn about electronics now." Beth asked her if she wanted to learn about electronics. The woman responded with a very strong no. Beth then told her what she did when her children wanted to learn things she was not willing to learn, she found tutors or instructional programs for her child.

As I have mentioned in other chapters, there are various people available in our communities who can help our children learn the things they want to know. If we feel we must do everything, then soon we will lose the ability to enjoy our child. Homeschooling then becomes drudgery. It is vital to reassess if this begins to happen.

Another component of preventing burn-out is setting priorities. Just why am I homeschooling? What is it that I am trying to accomplish? With the answers to these questions, we can look at the activities that engage us and sort them out in order of priority. It is easy to get caught up in a whirlwind of activity and find yourself continuing things that are no longer of value just because you have done them before.

It can be helpful for the whole family to take time to sit and talk together about the activities everyone participates in and the reason for those activities. It can help family members have a new appreciation for each other during intense times - such as end of the year dance recitals.

When I had three boys playing baseball, I asked for help with some of the daily kitchen chores because I was overwhelmed. My boys could see that I needed the help, and we worked out a schedule. Taking time to discuss things as a family helps all members of the family work together better.

Family discussion helps children to understand why they need to help out at certain times more than others. It can also help everyone in the family learn about what motivates different family members to do what they do. Learning to take time to assess one's motivation for doing something is a helpful lifelong skill. This leads into the next topic to help prevent burn-out: reevaluating one's activities and commitments.

As I mentioned in the chapter about curriculum, it's OK to stop doing something that you have started to do. It is not one of life's rules that you must finish an activity once you've started it. One of the favorite comments elementary teachers made on report cards when I was going to school was "so and so does not finish the tasks he was assigned to do." We forget that when we homeschool, we set the agenda. If we decide half way through that this is not the way we want to keep going, it is only sensible to stop.

My boys played baseball for about three years. For Noah, baseball was a very important activity. After the baseball season was over the year that he was 13, Noah worked very hard to build strength in his arm and shoulder muscles so that he would be an even better pitcher. One month before the start of baseball season and just before Noah turned 14, he was diagnosed with Type I Diabetes. He lost many pounds and all the muscles he had worked so hard to develop. Two weeks after he came home from the hospital, he attended baseball tryouts. After the tryouts, he decided that baseball wasn't worth the hassle it would involve arranging his schedule of meals and insulin injections to coincide with the games. The hassle did not balance out the fun of playing baseball. I was surprised by his decision as baseball had been so important to him.

Robin made a decision to stop playing baseball after playing on a 10 year old tournament team. He found that although he enjoyed playing (and he played well), he was distressed by the expectations one of the coaches had for his son. Robin decided that baseball wasn't fun enough to be worth the distress he felt watching adults hassle their children. This was not an easy decision for him as he had some very mixed feelings.

When I find myself reading the end of a book to see how it resolves, I realize that either I am bored by the book and I stop reading it, or I am not sure I will agree with the ending. Rather than spend my time reading the whole thing, I read the end first. It certainly surprises me to find myself doing this. I was sure that I had to read a book from start to finish once I started it. I can see how silly this idea is - it is a reader's choice after all to read a book in whatever order or sequence that appeals. It may make more sense to start at the beginning and read to the end, but there is no law written anywhere that says that this is the way it must be done. And if there were, how could it be enforced? Picturing a book police force in my mind, checking all the readers of the world helps me to laugh about other things I think I must do in a certain order or from start to finish. It helps me to remember that I am in charge.

At the same time that it is important to change when an activity or project no longer suits us, we need to consider the other people who may be involved when we change. Robin continued until the end of the tournament season. He could manage to play that long but he didn't want to play anymore after that. He can remember how glad he was that the team didn't win their tournament and go on to play more baseball. At the same time, he played his best because he wanted to feel good about his playing. Finding a balance between our commitment to ourselves and our commitment to others requires time and thought. Some situations are easy to resolve. Others, such as changing the way we educate our children, take more time.

Some families start homeschooling after years of school because children are unhappy and not learning even though parents may have made a commitment to making school work. Some children start going to school after being homeschooled because circumstances have changed even though parents were committed to homeschooling. We need to give ourselves permission to change; to no longer take part in things that we thought defined us.

Families that homeschool may homeschool for the entire 12 schooling years of a child's life or for a portion thereof. Some families decide after a few years of homeschooling that their children would benefit from going to school. Others decide to homeschool after a time spent in school. There is no one "right" way.

When a choice is made to change, it may seem as though the first choice made was wrong. In the case of sending a child to school after homeschooling, you might feel as though the only way to justify making the change from homeschooling to schooling is by thinking that you were wrong to homeschool in the first place; to deny the validity of what you did at home. I think it's important to keep in mind that homeschooling does not invalidate schooling nor does schooling invalidate homeschooling. There are many ways of meeting children's needs for education. I like to imagine that finding education suitable for a child and family is like going to a shoe store. No one would expect that every child would wear the same size or style of shoe. Feet are so individual. Our children's educational needs are individual, too.

When we make a change like changing from homeschooling to schooling, we may feel sheepish. We may feel that those who disagreed with our decision in the first place were right all along. This is difficult to face. What has helped me in situations like this is to try to see beyond black and white and see the gray areas when making a decision. Like finding shoes for one's child, finding the appropriate method of education is acknowledging change and growth. You would never expect your child to wear the same size or style of shoes at the age of 12 as he wore when he was 2 years old - his feet are different.

When you change from homeschooling to schooling or vice versa you are saying that things have changed. It could be your personal circumstances; it could be a child's request; it could be any number of things, but things have changed. It is more damaging to hold on to an idea that will no longer work for either you or your child or deny that a change in your circumstances, attitude, or ability has happened than to change. Your method of schooling your child at one time fit your circumstances as best as you could determine. Now, the foot has grown and it must be fit with a new shoe. Sometimes that means a big change - homeschooling to school or vice versa - or it could be a small change - trying a new method of homeschooling such as correspondence courses or "unschooling" when you have been following a set curriculum of studies.

If you make a change, be honest and clear to your child about the reasons. If there is no choice, then do not expect that the reasons you give your child will make the change easier. He or she may be experiencing a lot of different feelings from rage to relief. However, if you are honest with your child about the reasons, and word those reasons so that no blame is attached to the child (in other words, you own responsibility for the change) then at least your child knows where he stands. In some cases, it is a child who initiates the change from homeschooling to school or the other way around and it may be the parent who needs time to adjust.

If a child initiates the desire for change remember what I wrote about in the previous chapter regarding taking responsibility for age appropriate decisions. I, personally, would have a very difficult time letting a child under the age of 12 or 13 make a decision to go to school. It feels to me that a child of this age would not have enough information or life-experience to make such a decision.

If this kind of change happens in your family, give yourself time to adjust. It takes at least 6 months to accommodate a major lifestyle change. Major change is not easy. It requires a willingness to trust in the process of life and growth. We can often accept change that takes place within a certain framework, i.e., we expect our children to change from crawling babies to 10 year olds who can ride bikes, but we often barricade ourselves from change that goes beyond our framework of how life is supposed to be, i.e., a child who likes school after having been homeschooled. It is uncomfortable because it is discontinuous change rather than just an incremental change.

The same discomfort may exists when a child is homeschooled after being in school. It is an unexpected change that takes time to fit into our world view.

When children become learners at home instead of going to school, it may take quite a while before everyone is comfortable with the change. At first, a child may be happy to no longer have the pressure of school, then boredom may set in. It may be tempting to decide that "Augh!! This isn't working!" especially when a child is frustrated and complains about things. Give it time. Both you and your child need to learn new ways of being together, new expectations of each other, and how to work together.

The same applies if you are changing from homeschooling to having your children in school. You may doubt the wisdom of your decision, especially if your children express unhappiness. You may also doubt all that you did at home, if your child likes school. It will take time for all of you to adjust to this new pattern in your lives. Give it time.

I hope that what I have written helps you to have the courage to listen to your heart about meeting your children's educational needs and to make changes if they are needed. While I have chosen to homeschool my children for all of their schooling years, I realize that not all mothers who chose to homeschool will chose to homeschool for as long as I have or in the ways that I have. That, I see is one of the strengths of homeschooling - it's flexibility.

Moving back to burn-out, one thing that I have found very important to prevent burn-out is developing a life of my own. Homeschooling doesn't mean you must devote every moment of your life to your children. "Yes," I can hear you say, "but how do I find the time?" I wish I could give you an easy to follow recipe but there isn't one.

The following are some suggestions that have worked for some women. Before trying any of them, take time to look at the inner conflict that you may find when you take time for yourself. We carry around so many images of what it means to be a woman, a mother, a homeschooling mother. They are often in opposition to what it means to be a woman who has her own life.

My volunteer work with La Leche League gave me a place to use my talents while not taking me physically away from my children. Not very many organizations recognize that while it is important for a mother to have a life of her own, it is also vital that she not give up her life as a mother to have that life of her own. My volunteer work as a La Leche League Leader meant I could lead discussion groups with my babies and small children present, stopping to tend to their needs as necessary. As my children grew older and weren't happy attending meetings, I switched jobs. I did a job that involved a lot of correspondence. I could write or read my mail as I sat at the playground while my children played or as I sat in the stands while they participated in sports activities.

Mothers have just as great a need to be with their babies and toddlers as those babies and toddlers have a need to be with their mothers. We were meant to form attachments to our children. It is only while actually taking care of and mothering our babies and toddlers that we learn how to mother. Our society has a difficult time with attachment. As a culture, we are so terribly afraid of intimacy that we place an inordinate value on independence in young children. We belittle the attachment of children to their mothers with phrases like "Mama's boy," "tied to her apron strings," etc. We encourage mothers to find their own lives away from their children. Never imagining or realizing until it is too late that when we encourage mothers in this way, we encourage mothers to distance themselves from their children and thereby deny a vital part of themselves. (This topic - the importance and value of mothering for a woman who is a mother - is beyond the scope of this book. It is a subject that passionately interests me and will form the basis of my next book.)

Let's look at some of the ways to develop our lives that don't require separation from our children. Reading, both to myself and aloud to my children, helped me to take mini-vacations each day. Good books gave me a chance to view the world from another perspective. Reading allows me to enter a different space and keeps me sane. Even with four small children, I always found time to read to myself. It was absolutely vital for my survival.

Other women I know enjoy doing needlework. They say it gives them a sense of peace and relaxation that helps them to slow down after a day of meeting children's needs. Still others write in journals or on their computers to satisfy their need for time to themselves. Some women find that running or going for a walk can also give them a lift. A kitchen timer is a helpful tool here. Set the timer before going out the door to help your child know when you will be back and make sure you return at that time. (This assumes that there is an adult or teenager available to take care of younger children.)

Some women use the time that they are waiting while their children attend a class to do whatever it is that fills their need to have time for themselves. They do needle work, knit, read, write in journals, etc. It is uninterrupted time - you don't have to answer the phone. If you have more than one child and one child is with you while the other is attending a class, you could use this time as special time with this child -reading, playing card games, talking or going for a walk.

Another important part of preventing burn-out is to have a support system as I mentioned in the first chapter. You may find that your support system changes as your needs change. That's only to be expected. At one time in your life as a homeschooling mother, it may be very important to be in touch with other homeschooling women. At other times, you may find that you have no interest in this. Like those imaginary book police checking up to see if everyone is reading a book from start to finish, there is no one out there dictating to you how to find your support.

Overload is a common characteristic shared by all mothers. I hope that my suggestion that you develop your own life doesn't cause you more stress and conflict. I do not want to create the impression that as well as homeschooling your children, you should become a writer, an artist, an embroidery specialist, a marathon runner, or anything else. Homeschooling itself will be one way of developing your life. My intent in this chapter was to give you some ideas for preventing burn-out, not to cause it.

To close this chapter, here are some tension releasers that I've found helpful over the years.

Tensions Releasers:

1. Make sure that everyone has had something to eat or drink recently, including yourself.

2. Go outside. Being in the natural world often calms young and old alike. Going to the beach has been one of my favorite ways to restore myself. Hearing the birds and the sound of the waves as they reach the shore, seeing the light on the water, the flotsam and jetsam on the beach, my children playing in the sand and the large expanse of water helps me to breathe more deeply. At the same time being by the beach helps me to be in touch with something bigger than myself. It gives me perspective.

3. Engage in some sort of physical activity - dancing in the living room, running outside, skipping rope, stretching, yoga, playing soccer, baseball, basketball, croquet, etc.

4. Blow bubbles.

5. Take time to meditate, pray or visualize. I do this in the morning while I shower instead of in the evening because I used to fall asleep then. Doing some sort of visualization, meditation while I shower helps me stay grounded during the day. My favorite is a shortened version taken from the book *Ask Your Angels* by Alma

Daniel, Timothy Wyllie, and Andrew Ramer. I imagine roots coming out of the bottom of my feet and legs going into the ground, through the floor of the shower, the room below until the roots reach into the earth beneath my house and then down into the center of the earth. I then breath the energy of the earth up through my roots and into my heart. As I exhale, I send that energy pumping through my blood stream from my heart. I do this for three or four breaths and then imagine long filaments, like branches, reaching up from the top of my head and shoulders out past the roof and through the atmosphere to the stars. I then breath the energy of the stars into my heart and exhale that energy through my blood stream from my heart for three or four breaths. Then, I imagine energy coming from both the center of the earth and the stars into my heart and being pumped around by my heart. I find this exercise helps me to be centered. If I still have time and feel like it, I then surround myself with pink roses, below, above, beside, in front of and behind me before I open my eyes and finish showering.

When I forget to meditate for too long, I begin to lose touch with myself. Now that my children are older, I have time to meditate. However it is not built into my day as it was when they were babies and toddlers. The quiet times when I breastfed my babies and toddlers were the beginning of my regular meditation times. There is something very soothing for mom and babe alike when breastfeeding. I found it centered and calmed me. (That wonderful hormone prolactin!) Meditating has the same effect for me now but I have to remember to do it. When I had a nursing baby, the baby would remind me.

6. Don't "should" on your self! Let go of those preconceived notions that a mother should ...always be patient ...have fresh cookies available ...have all the laundry sorted and folded as soon as it's washed ...provide an interesting and challenging learning atmosphere all the time ...answer all the questions that children ask. Choose activities for your own reasons. Let go of the guilt of the "shoulds."

7. Get enough sleep! (Is this a should?)

8. Take time to enjoy your children! Look them in the eye and see the love that you share.

To close this chapter here's a quote I saw on the desk of a church secretary:

Do not feel totally, ultimately, and completely responsible for everything. That's my job!
Thanks, God

At the beach, 1989

And an old Scottish saying:

Angels fly because they take themselves lightly!

Holly 1990

CHAPTER 9
Conclusion:
Beyond Homeschooling

No book on homeschooling would be complete without looking at what happens after homeschooling.   Can someone who homeschools go to college or university? get a job? succeed in life? Yes. Homeschooling will not jeopardize your child's chances of finding work nor will it jeopardize his or her acceptance to an institution of higher learning. You and your child may need to do some extra work to demonstrate aptitude, ability and competency, but homeschooling does not close doors to jobs or further education. In fact, from what I have observed, young people who have been homeschooled have a sense of self-confidence and poise that will help them in any field they choose to pursue.

The concerns you have about higher education or job possibilities when you have a 6 year old are going to be different than the concerns you will have when that child is 16 years old. Over the subsequent years of homeschooling, your child will develop many interests and abilities. You will have the chance to facilitate the development of those interests.

If your child is interested in attending a college or university and shows proficiency in reading, writing, and the ability to do math, then entrance to post-secondary education institutions can be achieved. You and your child will more than likely need to spend time documenting competency and ability.

Here are some suggestions of how to document aptitude, ability and competency:

1. Start by finding out if the institution your child is interested in attending requires a high school transcript.

2. Does this institution accept portfolios of work - such as written work, art work, audio tapes, videotapes, etc. that demonstrate competence in a certain field instead of a high school transcript?

3. Does this institution use standardized college aptitude tests?

4. Will this institution administer tests to determine competency levels of students?

5. Will this institution accept a GED (general education degree)?

    a. If so, does your community offer high school equivalency tests?

    b. What age does a person need to be to take this test?

Libraries usually have books with sample high school equivalency tests. I was curious about these tests and checked a copy out of our library. The sample tests were all multiple choice. I wanted my children to know how to take multiple choice tests so I used these tests as a learning tool. We discovered that what was most important when taking these tests was knowing how to read for information and how to think critically. Even though some of the material in the tests was not familiar, the tests had enough explanatory information to make it possible to answer the questions. What was important in this test was the ability to comprehend the material presented and be able to refer to it to answer the questions - comprehension and critical thinking. My children found these tests easy to do. Even the youngest members of the family, who were between 7-11 at the time, could answer many of the questions.

The Scholastic Aptitude Test (SAT) or a similar test such as the National Merit Scholarship Qualifying Test (NMSQT) are a different matter. Many institutions use the scores of these tests as a gage of a student's aptitude for college level work. The SAT does not have the same kind of explanatory material as the high school equivalency test because it tests for verbal and mathematical aptitude rather than comprehension. Books of sample SAT tests are available in most libraries. SAT tests can help you establish a homeschooled child's aptitude to do college/university level work.   Keep in mind that these tests have a certain bias.   See the book *None of the Above: Behind the Myth of Scholastic Aptitude* by David Owen for an in depth look at the SAT.

Many high schools in the U. S. offer the SAT test in both the fall and spring to their grade 11 and 12 students. If you are interested in having your child take this test, check with your local public high school to find out how your child can take this test. If your child decides to take an SAT test, help him/her by setting up practice test situations with time periods and old SAT tests. The experience gained from these practice sessions will make it easier to take the actual test.

Trade and technical schools can be approached in the same way as colleges or universities. Find out what kind of documentation they need to admit a homeschooled student. Ask if they are flexible in their requirements for admission?

And What About College? How Homeschooling Can Lead to Admissions to the Best Colleges & Universities by Cafi Cohen has a lot of information that you may find helpful as you and your son and daughter explore post-secondary education.

Bear's Guide to Earning College Degrees Nontraditionally and this site on the internet http://www.virtualstudent.com/ might be helpful to you as you explore the options for higher education.   The Canadian Home Based Learning Organization has a list on their web site of Canadian colleges and universities and their policies for accepting homeschooled students. Their URL is: http://www.flora.org/homeschool-ca/

Keep in mind as you explore the possibilities of higher education that acquiring information is no longer tied to a specific location. As I mentioned in chapter 7, computer technology has changed our lives in ways that we have yet to acknowledge. Your child can use this technology to acquire post-secondary degrees. Just as you have educated your child in a nontraditional way by helping your child to learn at home, you and your child can explore various options for college or university. It doesn't have to be four years spent in one location, going to classes, and then graduating, although some students do choose to do this.

Something else to consider is early admittance to community college programs. Some community colleges will take students in their early teens as long as they have passed certain entrance requirements. Keep in mind that earlier doesn't necessarily mean better.

Those who go on to college or university after learning at home may find it a challenge at first. For some students the pace in college or university courses may be too slow and tedious, for others it may look confusing, especially if very little formal studying has been done previously. It may be helpful to encourage your college student to take less than a full course load at first. Your support and encouragement during this time in your child's life is just as vital as before.

Not every homeschooling child will want or need to go to college or university. One of the important things to do during the later teen years is to encourage your teenager to discover just what fields interest him or her. You can then explore together what sort of work is available in those fields and how to go about entering those fields. One homeschooler that I know wants to do something in the field of dance. She asked each of her dance teachers-ballet, folk, Hawaiian, tap, jazz, and flamingo - what the possibility was for her to become a professional dancer in that field. She then asked each of them what other possibilities there were if she could not be a professional dancer. Each of her teachers responded with a lot of information. One teacher told her about the field of dance notation - a field that needs more people. This opened up a field of study that she had not known about before.

When a homeschooled young adult applies for a job, it is just as important to document ability, competency, special interests or talents as it is for entrance to college, university, or a technical program. What is most important to any employer is whether or not the person applying for the job can do the work and is reliable enough to do the work. Documents that demonstrate reliability and responsibility are valuable references. Be resourceful when writing a résumé. Use experiences, a portfolio, an audio or video tape to demonstrate competency, ability, and willingness to learn new skills.

I hope this gives you a glimpse into the possibilities after homeschooling. Once a person is beyond the traditional schooling years, schooling methods are not as important as aptitude, ability, and commitment. If you have helped your children master the basics of reading, writing, and arithmetic, then they will be able to acquire other skills as needed.

Homeschooling can lead your family in directions you never expected. When children learn in nontraditional ways, they can also think in nontraditional ways. A number of people have commented to me how struck they have been by my children's originality and creative thinking abilities: "each child is unique, not one is a cookie cutter version of the other."

I think the world can use as many creative and original thinkers as possible. People who can see around what has always been done to find new ways to do things are in short supply. I think of my friend's son (who was homeschooled), who was enrolled in a work study program in computer engineering at a university. During one of his work terms, he read carefully through the waiver he was being asked to sign, and said he wouldn't sign it. The waiver not only waived ownership of work done for the company, but also past and future work that might be done on one's own. The boss asked him why he wouldn't sign, so he explained. The form was redesigned. This young man also noticed that some of the work that people needed to do was not being done very efficiently, and asked if he could do some reprogramming to fix this. He told his boss that he had extra time and it wouldn't interfere with his own work. He was given permission and went ahead and fixed it. Throughout the next day various workers came to the boss and asked what happened - work that used to take them 45 minutes to do, now only took 10 minutes. The boss explained. The boss offered this young man a full time position as soon as he graduated.

Not every child who homeschools will be a computer genius. However, when children are learning at home in non-regimented ways, they have the opportunity to observe and draw conclusions on their own, often leading to creative and original thinking. I once read "stupidity" defined as "continuing to do the same things in the same way and expecting a different outcome." My brother pointed out to me after reading the first edition of this book that if you reverse the thinking of this statement, it is the scientific method - "doing something in the same way should have the same outcome."

New ways of thinking and new ways of looking at things are desperately needed today. Children who have had the opportunity to think for themselves, to discover and explore the world at their own pace may grow up to be adults who are able to find new insights into old problems. I am always astonished by the astute observations that my children often have about things.

Let me give you an example. I described an incident from a book I had read recently - *Raising Cain: Protecting the Emotional Life of Boys* by Dan Kindlon, Ph.D. and Michael Thompson, Ph.D. - to one of my children. This incident involved a boy who had punched a hole in the wall of his bedroom. His mother sent him to the school psychologist (one of the authors) because she couldn't figure out what was making her son so angry. The psychologist eventually got the boy to talk. It turned out he wasn't angry, he was sad. It took a lot of work on the part of the psychologist before the boy trusted him enough to open up and share his sadness. One of my children made the following comments. "Anger gets results. Sadness doesn't. When this boy was a baby, probably his parents didn't respond to his nighttime crying. So he learned that when he was sad, nobody paid any attention. Parents teach their children that sad doesn't get a response. Anger, smashing walls, is different - it gets a response."

What an insightful observation! The authors of this book took many pages to say basically the same thing - how important it is to be responsive to your children, to give them reason to trust you by listening to them and to demonstrate your love by your actions.

My children often make comments like these in our discussions. They offer a fresh perspective or unexpected perception. These comments that my children share with me often opens doors in my mind that I didn't even know were closed.   One of the reasons I didn't want to send my children away from home for six hours a day is that I wanted to hear their observations, the conclusions they drew about what they had seen or observed. This is one of the best parts of homeschooling for me.

In closing, let me state again that homeschooling is not a panacea that will cure any or all of the ills of education. Deciding to homeschool is a commitment to a process of education that takes a tremendous amount of time and effort. It requires an alertness and awareness that can at times be draining, yet those who have done it find that the work involved is more than balanced by the rewards.

Let me quote two women whose homeschooled children are now in their late teens and twenties. I asked them, "Tell me about some of the benefits that you have received from homeschooling your children?" They answered:

"The closeness of my relationship to my children. My daughter and I are much closer than I was to my mother at her age. My daughter and I have shared so much together."

"I have grown up with my children. I was there while they were growing up so that I know them. Some women I know seem to be afraid of their older children. They don't know who they are."

"I worked hard to help my children reach their potential, so in the process I had to discover my own. In order for me to help them reach their potential, I had to model reaching for mine. I am doing things now that I never imagined I would be doing in the world of fashion. I never thought I would win a trip to Paris!"

"By making an unusual choice in educating my children, by 'bucking the system,' I have gained confidence to pursue ideas or ways of doing things that are unusual in other fields."

"By being at home and homeschooling my children, I was myself. If my children had gone to school, I would have gone back to work as a teacher. I would never have belonged to myself."

"I still get butterflies in my stomach when I think about how exciting it (homeschooling) is even now."

Being a homeschooling mother requires a commitment to your children and yourself to create a learning environment that is safe as well as stimulating. It requires a commitment to take the time and make the effort to nurture and support your children as they grow. It means building a caring and intimate relationship with your child. It will require all that you have to give and more. And yet, what else would you want to give?

Your life may change in ways that you do not expect: I never imagined I would perform as a children's entertainer in a shopping mall to help make payments on the loan for Josh's harp. I never imagined I would write a book about homeschooling, although writing has always been of interest to me. Not only have my children done things that delight and surprise me, I have delighted myself by the skills I have developed and strengthened as I helped my children to learn at home.

Teaching a child at home requires time, patience, and love. It requires humbleness, a willingness to wait, and a deep trust in the natural process of growth - your child's and your own. At any one moment, it may not seem as though learning is taking place. Then, all of a sudden, like the sun coming from behind a cloud, the new-found knowledge shines.

If you enjoy your child and have "butterflies" of excitement thinking about how much you'd like to try homeschooling, then do it. You and your child are about to start on an exciting adventure!

Afterword to the Revised Edition 2000:

I recently told a woman who was ordering copies of *Learning At Home: A Mother's Guide To Homeschooling* for her store that there would soon be a new revised edition. "Why are you revising it?" she asked. "It's wonderful the way it is."

Needless to say, her comment warmed my heart. I revised the book because I wanted to correct the typos, correct the font it was printed in, make the margins bigger, include a few more pictures and add a few things in various places. Writing, revising, publishing, and marketing this book continues what I started by choosing to help my children learn at home rather than sending them to school. I wonder what comes next?

Acknowledgments for the revised edition 2000

I wish to express my thanks to all the readers of the first edition of this book who wrote to me. Your notes telling me how much this book meant to you were an unexpected delight.

Acknowledgments from the first edition 1998

I wish to express my thanks to: Denise Green for her support and encouragement as I wrote this book. Her willingness to listen and give me feedback as I thought things out was invaluable. My son, Josh, for his time and thoughts about various parts of this book as well as help with the computer. My son, Noah, for his encouragement as well as help with graphics. My son, Robin, for listening to some of the chapters as I read them aloud to him late one night. My daughter, Holly, for her patience and willingness to wait while I wrote just a few more sentences. My husband, Larry, for his support and encouragement.

APPENDIX I

Read Aloud Books Not Mentioned Elsewhere

Burch, Robert: *Ida Early Comes Over The Mountain; Christmas With Ida Early*   for ages 6-8 and up

Godden, Rumer: *Didokai* for ages 9 and up; *Holly and Ivy* for ages 4 and up; *Home is the Sailor* for ages 6-7 and up; other books by this author

Erickson, Russell E.: *Warton and Morton; A Toad For Tuesday; Warton and The Castaways; Warton and The Contest; Warton and The King Of The Skies; Warton's Christmas Eve Adventure* for ages 4 and up

Goodall, Jane: *My Life With The Chimpanzees* for ages 10-12 and up

King-Smith, Dick: *Harry's Mad, The Cuckoo Child, Sheep Pig, Pigs Might Fly* and others for ages 5 and up

Lewis, C.S.: The Narnia Series for age 6-7 and up

Lindgren, Astrid: *The Brothers' Lionheart* for ages 7-8 and up

Paulsen, Gary: *Hatchet* and other books ages 11-12 and up

Streatfield, Noel: *Ballet Shoes; Apple Bough* ages 9 and up

Trease, Geoffrey: *Bows Against The Barons* ages 8-9 and up; *Cue For Treason* ages 9-10 and up; and other books

APPENDIX II

Goal Setting

1. **Current Activities:** List what you (or your family) are doing now – include all activities such as purchasing food, clothes, etc., cleaning house, reading stories, etc.   If you are working with others, share your lists and add to your own if appropriate. Set these aside, temporarily.

(3 min.)

2. **Needs/Wants:** Quietly, individually, reflect on your (or your family's) needs or wants.   Visualize the perfect situation and what you need to create that situation.

(1 min.)

3. **Sharing Needs/Wants:** List – on a flip chart, blackboard, or large piece of paper – the needs/wants that you and/or each person in the group has visualized.

(5 min.)

4. **Choosing Goals:** You have three stars (if you are working in a group, each person has three stars) to use to vote for what needs or wants are most important.   You can put all three in one place, one on each of three different places, or however you want to use your three stars.   After everyone has voted with their stars, pick the three needs with the most stars.   From these choose one.   This now becomes your goal.

(2-5 min.)

5. **Writing And Sharing An Objective Goal Statement:** Write a statement about the goal you have just selected that tells exactly what you want to accomplish.   Be as specific as possible (include numbers, dates, etc.) so that you can measure or observe your progress toward achieving your goal.   If you are working with someone else, share this statement with them.   Here's an example.   Let's

say that you have as your goal to be more patient because you are not happy that you are losing your temper 4 or more times a day. An objective statement would be - I will increase my patience by 25% by the end of 60 days. I will not lose my temper more than three times a day.

(5-10 min.)

6.   **Brainstorming Possibilities:** List all ideas that can help you achieve your goal. Remember, when you are brainstorming – any idea is valid no matter how unlikely, impossible, or silly it may seem. Record without judgment. Using the example, here's a list of brainstorming ideas about increasing one's patience:

1. Get a patience transplant
2. Have hired help to do the wash, clean the house, cook all the food, etc.
3. Take a nap everyday
4. Have your children take naps every day
5. Have Mary Poppins come and entertain your children twice a week
6. Learn hypnotism, so that you can hypnotize yourself to be more patient
7. Hypnotize your children so that they do not do things that call on your patience
8. Purchase a tank of nitrous oxide, laughing gas, to use when you are on the edge
9. Reduce the number of activities family members participate in

(5-10 Min.)

7.   **Action Steps:** Using the brainstorming list in combination with the first list that you made (current activities), pick out those items that will be most effective in accomplishing your goal.   Under the items that you choose, list specific steps that you will take.

Using the example: If you have listed that you have too much house work and run out of patience when your children want you to read a story, you might consider getting a neighborhood teenager to come and read stories to your children while you do a house-cleaning blitz. Or you may decide to hire a neighborhood teenager to clean the bathroom and do a number of loads of laundry while you read to your children. You may not be able to afford full time help, but you can find ways to lessen your burden.   Sometimes, women get together and share housework, while one mother reads or plays games with all the children. These and other ideas can come out in the brainstorming session.

8. **Time Table:** Working backwards from your target date or perhaps an event, build a time table for the action steps you have listed. This is more useful as a step in goal setting when you have a specific event or goal you want to accomplish such as planning a birthday party or another celebration. For more general life style changes, a time table may cause stress. The intention of goal setting is to relieve stress.   Don't let the time table or your action steps get in the way of enjoying your life.

Using the example, you may decide that in a month's time after using the new approaches you have outlined, you will reassess the goals you set and the ways in which you implemented those goals.

9. **Assignments:** Decide for each step in the action plan who will do what by when. This is a very critical part when planning with a group or more than one person. It is important for each person to know who is going to do what when, in order to implement any changes. This is also a time to set up when the action plan will be reviewed.

This goal setting and action planning method can be used to help children decide what they want to do by modifying the technique so that it is appropriate for their age. You could ask children to draw a picture on a card that describes the activities that they want to do −a different card for each activity. Then you can look at those cards together and ask your child to put them in order of what they most want to do to least want to do (priorize them). You can then discuss why these activities are important. From there you can brainstorm how to accomplish these goals.

We have done this without the step of drawing the activities on cards because the activities my children wanted to participate in were few. We did not need the visual aid that cards provided.

APPENDIX III

Homeschooling Sources Of Information

CANADA

http://www.flora.org/homeschool-ca/

The Canadian Home Based Learning Resource Page hosts the only national home based learning organization in Canada, ACHBE (Association of Canadian Home Based Education). The web site also provides listservs, discussion boards, and a student exchange program along with information about local regulations, support groups, and activities for every province and territory in Canada.

Note: ACHBE does not collect membership fees.

Please include a SASE (or $1.00) if you require a written response.

C/O J. Campbell
PO Box 34148, RPO Fort Richmond
Winnipeg, Manitoba   R3T 5T5
Fax (815) 366-5342
Email: homeschool-ca-admin@flora.org

USA

http://www.home-ed-magazine.com

Home Education Magazine PO Box 1083, Tonasket, WA   98855 This bimonthly glossy cover magazine has numerous articles by parents who homeschool their children as well as columns by experienced homeschooling parents. The web site has archives from the magazine plus "how to homeschool" information. Published by Mark and Helen Hegener, experienced homeschooling parents.

http://www.holtgws.com/

Growing Without Schooling 308 Boylston St., Boston, Mass. 02116 This is the organization and newsletter started by John Holt and continued by others since his death.

WORLDWIDE

Check the internet for more information about homeschooling. Try your local library.

APPENDIX IV

Playdough Recipe

1 cup of flour
2 tsp. cream of tartar
½ cup salt
2 Tbs. oil
1 cup of water
various food colors

Mix the dry ingredients. Add oil, water, and color of choice and stir. Cook for 3 minutes (use a timer) until the dough is the consistency of mashed potatoes. Use a different color for each batch or leave white if so desired. Knead with flour if needed. Store in covered containers in the refrigerator.

APPENDIX V

Making a Rope Ladder

Supplies needed:
2   1" diameter x 3' long dowel rods cut to 1 foot lengths
16' of ¼" nylon braid

You may wish to increase the dimensions of both the length of the dowel and the length of the rope between each dowel depending on the size of your child. These instructions will suit a child up to about age 7-9 years old.

1. Drill 1/4" holes one inch from the ends of the one foot dowel pieces.

2. Thread rope through holes in the first dowel, putting the middle of the rope in the middle of the dowel.

3. Tie knots in the rope over each hole.

4. Tie a knot 12" up on each side of the rope.

5. Thread each end of the rope through the next dowel rod, and tie a knot above the hole. Make sure the knot is bigger than the hole so that the rope does not slip through.

6. Continue in this manner, tying a knot 12" up on each side until all the dowel rods have been secured.

7. Hang with screw eyes or tie around a branch. Move knots around to level dowel rods.

8. Test ladder with adult weight for security before allowing a child to climb or swing on it.

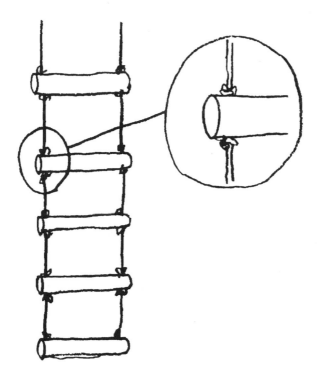

Bibliography

Chapter 1:
1. *The Day Care Decision: What's Best For Your Child?* by William and Wendy Dreskin
2. *How Children Learn; How Children Fail* by John Holt
3. *De-schooling Society* by Ivan Illich
4. *Your Child's Growing Mind* by Jane M. Healy, Ph.D.
5. *People Skills* by Robert Bolton
6. *How To Talk So Kids Will Listen And Listen So Kids Will Talk* by Adele Faber and Elaine Mazlish
7. *Mastering Your Hidden Self* by Serge King
8. *The Drama of the Gifted Child; For Your Own Good; Thou Shalt Not Be Aware; Banished Knowledge; Breaking the Wall of Silence* by Alice Miller
9. *Discipline: Kids Are Worth It* by Barbara Coloroso
10. *No Contest: The Case Against Competition* by Alfie Kohn
11. *Teach Only Love* by Gerald Jampolsky, M.D.

Chapter 2:
1. *How Tom Beat Captain Najork And His Hired Sportsmen* by Russell Hoban
2. *Truckers* by Terry Pratchett
3. *Women Who Run With The Wolves* by Clarisa Pinkola Estes
4. *For Your Own Good; Thou Shalt Not Be Aware, Banished Knowledge, Breaking the Wall of Silence* by Alice Miller
5. *How To Parent* by Fitzhugh Dodson
6. *How Children Learn* by John Holt
7. *How To Really Love Your Child* by Ross Campbell
8. *The World of Lego Toys* by Henry Wiencek
9. *Noah's Ark* by Rien Poortvliet

Chapter 3:
1. *Teacher* by Sylvia Ashton Warner
2. *The Read-Aloud Handbook* by Jim Trelease
3. *Bears on Wheels; The Honey Hunt; The Bears' Christmas* by Jan and Stan Berenstain

4. *More Spaghetti, I Say!* by Rita Gelman
5. *Charlotte's Web; The Trumpet of The Swan* by E.B. White
6. *Reading* by Bruno Bettleheim
7. *aha! Insight* by Martin Gardner
8. *The Art of Education* by Rudolph Steiner
9. *How Children Learn; How Children Fail; The Underachieving School; Instead of Education; Teach Your Own; Learning All the Time; It's Never Too Late* by John Holt
10. *Farmer's Alphabet* by Mary Azarian
11. *Little Bear; Little Bear's Visit; Little Bear's Friend; Little Bear's Father; A Kiss For Little Bear* by Else Minarik
12. *Tales of Oliver Pig; More Tales About Oliver; Tales of Amanda Pig; Oliver And Amanda's Christmas* by Jan Van Leeuwen
13. *Frog and Toad; Frog and Toad Are Friends; Frog and Toad All Year; Owl At Home* by Arnold Lobel
14. *Nate the Great; Nate the Great and the ...* by Marjorie Weinman Sharmat
15. *Why Johnny Can't Read; Why Johnny Still Can't Read* by Rudolph Flesch
16. *Games for Reading* by Peggy Kaye
17. *The Lives of Children* by George Dennison
18. *The Sounds of...* Readers by Bill Martin, Jr. (Holt Rinehart Winston Publishers)
19. *Teaching the Universe of Discourse* by James Moffett

Chapter 4:
1. *Grooks* by Piet Hein
2. *Brain Sex: The Real Difference Between Men and Women* by Anne Moire, Ph.D. and David Jessel
3. *Men Are From Mars, Women Are From Venus* by John Gray, Ph.D.
4. *Learning All the Time* by John Holt
5. *English Grammar and Composition* by John E. Warriner
6. *The Elements of Style* by William Strunk, Jr. and E.B. White
7. *The Well-Tempered Sentence - A Punctuation Handbook for the Innocent, the Eager, and the Doomed* by Karen Elizabeth Gordon
8. *How To Write Plain English* by Rudolph Flesch

Chapter 5:
1. *How Children Fail* by John Holt
2. *Stein's Refresher Mathematics* by Edwin Stein
3. *Arithmetic Made Simple* by A.T. Sperling and Samuel D. Levison
4. Books by Martin Gardner
5. *Mathematics, A Human Endeavor*, *Geometry*, *Algebra* by Harold Jacobs
6. Books by Piaget on child development
7. *Origami Made Easy*, *Creative Origami* by Kunihiko Kasahara
8. *Origami* by Paulo Mulatinho
9. *Classic Origami* by Paul Jackson
10. *The World of Origami* by Isao Honda
11. *Teachers and Machines: The Classroom Use of Technology Since 1920* (1986) by Larry Cuban
12. *Silicon Snake Oil: Second Thoughts on the Information Highway* (1995) by Clifford Stoll
13. *Endangered Minds: Why Children Can't Think and What We Can Do About It* (1990) by Jane Healy
14. *The End of Education* (1995) by Neil Postman
15. *Life On Screen: Identity in the Age of the Internet* (1995) by Sherry Turkle

Chapter 6
1. *Superlearning* by S. Ostrander and L. Schroeder
2. *Drawing on the Right Side of the Brain* by Betty Edwards
3. *The Natural Way to Draw* by Kimon Nicolaïdes
4. *Great Painters* by Piero Ventura
5. *Teddybears and How To Make Them* by Margaret Hutchings
6. *How To Raise A Healthy Child In Spite of Your Doctor* by Robert Mendelsohn, M.D.
7. *Homeopathic Medicine At Home* by Maesimand Panos, M. D. and Jane Heimlich
8. *The Plug-In Drug* by Marie Winn
9. *Lives of Musicians* by Kathleen Krull
10. *Bill Peet, an Autobiography* by Bill Peet
11. *Beethoven Lives Upstairs* by Classical Kids recordings
12. Storytellers:

a. Jay O'Callahan 1-800-626-5356 to order catalogue
http://www.ocallahan.com/
b. Doug Lipman P.O. Box 44195, West Sommerville, MA
02144   http://www.storypower.com/
c. Danny Kaye - *Stories From Around the World*; *Hans Christian Anderson*
d. National Storytellers Association, P.O. Box 309,
Jonesborough, Tenn. 37659 USA.
http://www.storytellingfoundation.net/home.htm
for storytelling festival information

Chapter 7

1. *If You Want To Be Rich and Happy, Don't Go To School* by Robert T. Kiyosaki
2. *Bingo Long and the Travelling All Stars* (film) book by William Brashler
3. *Misty of Chincoteague*; *Sea Star*; *Stormy*; *Misty's Foal* by Marguerite Henry
4. *I Love Guinea Pigs*; *Sheep Pig*; *Pigs Might Fly*; *Harry's Mad*; *The Cuckoo Child* by Dick King-Smith
5. *Bet You Can*; *Bet Can't* by Vicki Cobb
6. The Magic School Bus series by Joanna Cole
7. "The Wheel of the Water" song by Tom Chapin from *Mother Earth*
8. Eyewitness Jr. series published by Alfred Knopf
9. *Benny's Animals* by Millicent E. Selsam
10. *Richard Scarry's What Do People Do All Day*; *Great Big Air Book*
11. *Huck Scarry's Things That Fly*; *Things That Go*
12. *How we are BORN How we GROW How our bodies WORK and How we LEARN* by Joe Kaufman
13. *My Family and Other Animals* and other books by Gerald Durrell
14. *Absolute Zero Gravity* by Betsy Devine and Joel E. Cohen
15. *Surely Your Joking, Mr. Feynman!*; *What Do You Care What Other People Think* by Richard Feynman
16. *The Call of Stories* by Robert Coles
17. *Margaret By Herself*; *Margaret In The Middle*; *Margaret On Her Way* by Beatrice Hunter

18. *Cheaper by the Dozen*; *Belles on Their Toes* by Frank B. Gilbreth, Jr. and Ernestine Gilbreth Carey

19. *The Little House Books* by Laura Ingalls Wilder

20. The Rocky Ridge Years - *The Little House on Rocky Ridge*; *Little Farm in the Ozarks*; *In the Land of the Big Red Apple*; *On the Other Side of the Hill* by Roger McBride continues the Laura Ingalls Wilder books

21. *Anastatia Krupnik*; *Number the Stars* by Lois Lowry

22. *The Silver Sword* by Ian Serraillier

23. *The Good Master*; *The Singing Tree*; *The Chestry Oak* by Kate Seredy

24. *The House of Sixty Fathers* by Meindert de Jong

25. *Homecoming; Dicey's Song; Solitary Blue; Jackaroo* and other books by Cynthia Voigt

26. *Castle; City; Pyramid; Cathedral* by David Macaulay

27. *The Day the Universe Changed* by James Burke (both book and film series)

28. *The Living Planet* by David Attenborough (Video-film series) also available in book form

Chapter 8

1. *People Skills* by Robert Bolton

2. *The Win-Win Negotiator* by Ross R. Reck, Ph.D. and Brian G. Long, Ph.D.

3. *Dealing With People You Can't Stand* By Dr. Rick Brinkman and Dr. Rick Kirschner

4. *Dance of Anger; Dance of Intimacy* Harriet Lerner

5. *What's a Smart Woman Like You Doing At Home* by Linda Burton, Janet Dittmer, Cheri Loveless

6. *Ask Your Angels* by Alma Daniels, Timothy Wyllie, Andrew Ramer

7. *Emmanuel's Book* compiled by Pat Rodegast and Judith Stanton

Chapter 9

1. *Homeschooling For Excellence* by David and Micki Colfax

2. *And What About College? How Homeschooling Can Lead To Admission To The Best Colleges and Universities* by Cafi Cohen

3. *None of the Above; Behind The Myth of Scholastic Aptitude* by David

Owen

4. *John Bear's Guide to Non-traditional College Degrees; College Degrees By Mail and Modem* by John Bear

5. *Raising Cain: Protecting the Emotional Life Of Boys* by Dan Kindlon, Ph.D. and Michael Thompson, Ph.D.

Prime Time Parenting Series

by Marty Layne

Solving the Bed Time Blues
Suggestions for a calmer, more enjoyable transition to bedtime
(8 pages $1.50 US/$2.00 Canadian)

Reading Out Loud   Why it's important
                          How to do it
                          Suggestions for what to read
                          (8 pages $1.50 US/$2.00 Canadian)

Top Ten Things To Do On A Rainy Day
Fun activities for indoor play
Suggestions for having fun in the rain
          (8 pages $1.50 US/$2.00 Canadian)

Shipping is included in all prices for Canada and the US
Overseas orders, please add $0.50 US/Canadian per item.

Please send a check or money order made out to
          Sea Change Publications
          1850 San Lorenzo Ave.
          Victoria, BC V8N 2E9 Canada

Check our web site for new releases including audio recordings
for children and adults:
http://members.home.net/seachangepublications/

For information about recordings by Josh Layne go to
http:members.home.net/lbstudio/